C-2818

THIS IS YOUR **PASSBOOK**® FOR ...

TRAFFIC CHECKER

NATIONAL LEARNING CORPORATION®
passbooks.com

Copyright © 2018 by

National Learning Corporation

212 Michael Drive, Syosset, NY 11791
(516) 921-8888 • www.passbooks.com
E-mail: info@passbooks.com

PUBLISHED IN THE UNITED STATES OF AMERICA

PASSBOOK® SERIES

THE *PASSBOOK® SERIES* has been created to prepare applicants and candidates for the ultimate academic battlefield – the examination room.

At some time in our lives, each and every one of us may be required to take an examination – for validation, matriculation, admission, qualification, registration, certification, or licensure.

Based on the assumption that every applicant or candidate has met the basic formal educational standards, has taken the required number of courses, and read the necessary texts, the *PASSBOOK® SERIES* furnishes the one special preparation which may assure passing with confidence, instead of failing with insecurity. Examination questions – together with answers – are furnished as the basic vehicle for study so that the mysteries of the examination and its compounding difficulties may be eliminated or diminished by a sure method.

This book is meant to help you pass your examination provided that you qualify and are serious in your objective.

The entire field is reviewed through the huge store of content information which is succinctly presented through a provocative and challenging approach – the question-and-answer method.

A climate of success is established by furnishing the correct answers at the end of each test.

You soon learn to recognize types of questions, forms of questions, and patterns of questioning. You may even begin to anticipate expected outcomes.

You perceive that many questions are repeated or adapted so that you can gain acute insights, which may enable you to score many sure points.

You learn how to confront new questions, or types of questions, and to attack them confidently and work out the correct answers.

You note objectives and emphases, and recognize pitfalls and dangers, so that you may make positive educational adjustments.

Moreover, you are kept fully informed in relation to new concepts, methods, practices, and directions in the field.

You discover that you arre actually taking the examination all the time: you are preparing for the examination by "taking" an examination, not by reading extraneous and/or supererogatory textbooks.

In short, this PASSBOOK®, used directedly, should be an important factor in helping you to pass your test.

TRAFFIC CHECKER

DUTIES

As a Traffic Checker, you will be collecting data relating to ridership, performance and travel patterns on the bus and subway routes, which includes counting the number of passengers going up and down subway entrances and exits, number of passengers on a bus, total number of passengers on a particular subway car, and taking turnstile readings. You will hand out survey forms and distribute promotional and informational materials to passengers as well as monitor environmental and aesthetic factors throughout the system. You will be required to work outdoors in all kinds of weather.

SCOPE OF THE EXAMINATION

The <u>written test</u> will cover knowledge, skills and/or abilities in such areas as:

1. Data collection and analysis;
2. Map reading;
3. Name and number checking;
4. Arithmetic reasoning;
5. Understanding and interpreting tabular material;
6. Filling out forms; and
7. Interacting with the public.

HOW TO TAKE A TEST

I. YOU MUST PASS AN EXAMINATION

A. *WHAT EVERY CANDIDATE SHOULD KNOW*

Examination applicants often ask us for help in preparing for the written test. What can I study in advance? What kinds of questions will be asked? How will the test be given? How will the papers be graded?

As an applicant for a civil service examination, you may be wondering about some of these things. Our purpose here is to suggest effective methods of advance study and to describe civil service examinations.

Your chances for success on this examination can be increased if you know how to prepare. Those "pre-examination jitters" can be reduced if you know what to expect. You can even experience an adventure in good citizenship if you know why civil service exams are given.

B. *WHY ARE CIVIL SERVICE EXAMINATIONS GIVEN?*

Civil service examinations are important to you in two ways. As a citizen, you want public jobs filled by employees who know how to do their work. As a job seeker, you want a fair chance to compete for that job on an equal footing with other candidates. The best-known means of accomplishing this two-fold goal is the competitive examination.

Exams are widely publicized throughout the nation. They may be administered for jobs in federal, state, city, municipal, town or village governments or agencies.

Any citizen may apply, with some limitations, such as the age or residence of applicants. Your experience and education may be reviewed to see whether you meet the requirements for the particular examination. When these requirements exist, they are reasonable and applied consistently to all applicants. Thus, a competitive examination may cause you some uneasiness now, but it is your privilege and safeguard.

C. *HOW ARE CIVIL SERVICE EXAMS DEVELOPED?*

Examinations are carefully written by trained technicians who are specialists in the field known as "psychological measurement," in consultation with recognized authorities in the field of work that the test will cover. These experts recommend the subject matter areas or skills to be tested; only those knowledges or skills important to your success on the job are included. The most reliable books and source materials available are used as references. Together, the experts and technicians judge the difficulty level of the questions.

Test technicians know how to phrase questions so that the problem is clearly stated. Their ethics do not permit "trick" or "catch" questions. Questions may have been tried out on sample groups, or subjected to statistical analysis, to determine their usefulness.

Written tests are often used in combination with performance tests, ratings of training and experience, and oral interviews. All of these measures combine to form the best-known means of finding the right person for the right job.

II. HOW TO PASS THE WRITTEN TEST

A. *NATURE OF THE EXAMINATION*

To prepare intelligently for civil service examinations, you should know how they differ from school examinations you have taken. In school you were assigned certain definite pages to read or subjects to cover. The examination questions were quite detailed and usually emphasized memory. Civil service exams, on the other hand, try to discover your present ability to perform the duties of a position, plus your potentiality to learn these duties. In other words, a civil service exam attempts to predict how successful you will be. Questions cover such a broad area that they cannot be as minute and detailed as school exam questions.

In the public service similar kinds of work, or positions, are grouped together in one "class." This process is known as *position-classification*. All the positions in a class are paid according to the salary range for that class. One class title covers all of these positions, and they are all tested by the same examination.

B. *FOUR BASIC STEPS*

1) Study the announcement

How, then, can you know what subjects to study? Our best answer is: "Learn as much as possible about the class of positions for which you've applied." The exam will test the knowledge, skills and abilities needed to do the work.

Your most valuable source of information about the position you want is the official exam announcement. This announcement lists the training and experience qualifications. Check these standards and apply only if you come reasonably close to meeting them.

The brief description of the position in the examination announcement offers some clues to the subjects which will be tested. Think about the job itself. Review the duties in your mind. Can you perform them, or are there some in which you are rusty? Fill in the blank spots in your preparation.

Many jurisdictions preview the written test in the exam announcement by including a section called "Knowledge and Abilities Required," "Scope of the Examination," or some similar heading. Here you will find out specifically what fields will be tested.

2) Review your own background

Once you learn in general what the position is all about, and what you need to know to do the work, ask yourself which subjects you already know fairly well and which need improvement. You may wonder whether to concentrate on improving your strong areas or on building some background in your fields of weakness. When the announcement has specified "some knowledge" or "considerable knowledge," or has used adjectives like "beginning principles of..." or "advanced ... methods," you can get a clue as to the number and difficulty of questions to be asked in any given field. More questions, and hence broader coverage, would be included for those subjects which are more important in the work. Now weigh your strengths and weaknesses against the job requirements and prepare accordingly.

3) Determine the level of the position

Another way to tell how intensively you should prepare is to understand the level of the job for which you are applying. Is it the entering level? In other words, is this the position in which beginners in a field of work are hired? Or is it an intermediate or advanced level? Sometimes this is indicated by such words as "Junior" or "Senior" in the class title. Other jurisdictions use Roman numerals to designate the level – Clerk I, Clerk II, for example. The word "Supervisor" sometimes appears in the title. If the level is not indicated by the title, check the description of duties. Will you be working under very close supervision, or will you have responsibility for independent decisions in this work?

4) Choose appropriate study materials

Now that you know the subjects to be examined and the relative amount of each subject to be covered, you can choose suitable study materials. For beginning level jobs, or even advanced ones, if you have a pronounced weakness in some aspect of your training, read a modern, standard textbook in that field. Be sure it is up to date and has general coverage. Such books are normally available at your library, and the librarian will be glad to help you locate one. For entry-level positions, questions of appropriate difficulty are chosen – neither highly advanced questions, nor those too simple. Such questions require careful thought but not advanced training.

If the position for which you are applying is technical or advanced, you will read more advanced, specialized material. If you are already familiar with the basic principles of your field, elementary textbooks would waste your time. Concentrate on advanced textbooks and technical periodicals. Think through the concepts and review difficult problems in your field.

These are all general sources. You can get more ideas on your own initiative, following these leads. For example, training manuals and publications of the government agency which employs workers in your field can be useful, particularly for technical and professional positions. A letter or visit to the government department involved may result in more specific study suggestions, and certainly will provide you with a more definite idea of the exact nature of the position you are seeking.

III. KINDS OF TESTS

Tests are used for purposes other than measuring knowledge and ability to perform specified duties. For some positions, it is equally important to test ability to make adjustments to new situations or to profit from training. In others, basic mental abilities not dependent on information are essential. Questions which test these things may not appear as pertinent to the duties of the position as those which test for knowledge and information. Yet they are often highly important parts of a fair examination. For very general questions, it is almost impossible to help you direct your study efforts. What we can do is to point out some of the more common of these general abilities needed in public service positions and describe some typical questions.

1) General information

Broad, general information has been found useful for predicting job success in some kinds of work. This is tested in a variety of ways, from vocabulary lists to questions about current events. Basic background in some field of work, such as sociology or economics, may be sampled in a group of questions. Often these are principles which have become familiar to most persons through exposure rather than through formal training. It is difficult to advise you how to study for these questions; being alert to the world around you is our best suggestion.

2) Verbal ability

An example of an ability needed in many positions is verbal or language ability. Verbal ability is, in brief, the ability to use and understand words. Vocabulary and grammar tests are typical measures of this ability. Reading comprehension or paragraph interpretation questions are common in many kinds of civil service tests. You are given a paragraph of written material and asked to find its central meaning.

3) Numerical ability

Number skills can be tested by the familiar arithmetic problem, by checking paired lists of numbers to see which are alike and which are different, or by interpreting charts and graphs. In the latter test, a graph may be printed in the test booklet which you are asked to use as the basis for answering questions.

4) Observation

A popular test for law-enforcement positions is the observation test. A picture is shown to you for several minutes, then taken away. Questions about the picture test your ability to observe both details and larger elements.

5) Following directions

In many positions in the public service, the employee must be able to carry out written instructions dependably and accurately. You may be given a chart with several columns, each column listing a variety of information. The questions require you to carry out directions involving the information given in the chart.

6) Skills and aptitudes

Performance tests effectively measure some manual skills and aptitudes. When the skill is one in which you are trained, such as typing or shorthand, you can practice. These tests are often very much like those given in business school or high school courses. For many of the other skills and aptitudes, however, no short-time preparation can be made. Skills and abilities natural to you or that you have developed throughout your lifetime are being tested.

Many of the general questions just described provide all the data needed to answer the questions and ask you to use your reasoning ability to find the answers. Your best preparation for these tests, as well as for tests of facts and ideas, is to be at your physical and mental best. You, no doubt, have your own methods of getting into an exam-taking mood and keeping "in shape." The next section lists some ideas on this subject.

IV. KINDS OF QUESTIONS

Only rarely is the "essay" question, which you answer in narrative form, used in civil service tests. Civil service tests are usually of the short-answer type. Full instructions for answering these questions will be given to you at the examination. But in case this is your first experience with short-answer questions and separate answer sheets, here is what you need to know:

1) Multiple-choice Questions

Most popular of the short-answer questions is the "multiple choice" or "best answer" question. It can be used, for example, to test for factual knowledge, ability to solve problems or judgment in meeting situations found at work.

A multiple-choice question is normally one of three types—

- It can begin with an incomplete statement followed by several possible endings. You are to find the one ending which *best* completes the statement, although some of the others may not be entirely wrong.
- It can also be a complete statement in the form of a question which is answered by choosing one of the statements listed.
- It can be in the form of a problem – again you select the best answer.

Here is an example of a multiple-choice question with a discussion which should give you some clues as to the method for choosing the right answer:

When an employee has a complaint about his assignment, the action which will *best* help him overcome his difficulty is to
   A. discuss his difficulty with his coworkers
   B. take the problem to the head of the organization
   C. take the problem to the person who gave him the assignment
   D. say nothing to anyone about his complaint

In answering this question, you should study each of the choices to find which is best. Consider choice "A" – Certainly an employee may discuss his complaint with fellow employees, but no change or improvement can result, and the complaint remains unresolved. Choice "B" is a poor choice since the head of the organization probably does not know what assignment you have been given, and taking your problem to him is known as "going over the head" of the supervisor. The supervisor, or person who made the assignment, is the person who can clarify it or correct any injustice. Choice "C" is, therefore, correct. To say nothing, as in choice "D," is unwise. Supervisors have and interest in knowing the problems employees are facing, and the employee is seeking a solution to his problem.

2) True/False Questions

The "true/false" or "right/wrong" form of question is sometimes used. Here a complete statement is given. Your job is to decide whether the statement is right or wrong.

SAMPLE: A roaming cell-phone call to a nearby city costs less than a non-roaming call to a distant city.

This statement is wrong, or false, since roaming calls are more expensive.
This is not a complete list of all possible question forms, although most of the others are variations of these common types. You will always get complete directions for

answering questions. Be sure you understand *how* to mark your answers – ask questions until you do.

V. RECORDING YOUR ANSWERS

Computer terminals are used more and more today for many different kinds of exams.

For an examination with very few applicants, you may be told to record your answers in the test booklet itself. Separate answer sheets are much more common. If this separate answer sheet is to be scored by machine – and this is often the case – it is highly important that you mark your answers correctly in order to get credit.

An electronic scoring machine is often used in civil service offices because of the speed with which papers can be scored. Machine-scored answer sheets must be marked with a pencil, which will be given to you. This pencil has a high graphite content which responds to the electronic scoring machine. As a matter of fact, stray dots may register as answers, so do not let your pencil rest on the answer sheet while you are pondering the correct answer. Also, if your pencil lead breaks or is otherwise defective, ask for another.

Since the answer sheet will be dropped in a slot in the scoring machine, be careful not to bend the corners or get the paper crumpled.

The answer sheet normally has five vertical columns of numbers, with 30 numbers to a column. These numbers correspond to the question numbers in your test booklet. After each number, going across the page are four or five pairs of dotted lines. These short dotted lines have small letters or numbers above them. The first two pairs may also have a "T" or "F" above the letters. This indicates that the first two pairs only are to be used if the questions are of the true-false type. If the questions are multiple choice, disregard the "T" and "F" and pay attention only to the small letters or numbers.

Answer your questions in the manner of the sample that follows:

32. The largest city in the United States is
    A. Washington, D.C.
    B. New York City
    C. Chicago
    D. Detroit
    E. San Francisco

1) Choose the answer you think is best. (New York City is the largest, so "B" is correct.)
2) Find the row of dotted lines numbered the same as the question you are answering. (Find row number 32)
3) Find the pair of dotted lines corresponding to the answer. (Find the pair of lines under the mark "B.")
4) Make a solid black mark between the dotted lines.

VI. BEFORE THE TEST

Common sense will help you find procedures to follow to get ready for an examination. Too many of us, however, overlook these sensible measures. Indeed, nervousness and fatigue have been found to be the most serious reasons why applicants fail to do their best on civil service tests. Here is a list of reminders:

- Begin your preparation early – Don't wait until the last minute to go scurrying around for books and materials or to find out what the position is all about.
- Prepare continuously – An hour a night for a week is better than an all-night cram session. This has been definitely established. What is more, a night a week for a month will return better dividends than crowding your study into a shorter period of time.
- Locate the place of the exam – You have been sent a notice telling you when and where to report for the examination. If the location is in a different town or otherwise unfamiliar to you, it would be well to inquire the best route and learn something about the building.
- Relax the night before the test – Allow your mind to rest. Do not study at all that night. Plan some mild recreation or diversion; then go to bed early and get a good night's sleep.
- Get up early enough to make a leisurely trip to the place for the test – This way unforeseen events, traffic snarls, unfamiliar buildings, etc. will not upset you.
- Dress comfortably – A written test is not a fashion show. You will be known by number and not by name, so wear something comfortable.
- Leave excess paraphernalia at home – Shopping bags and odd bundles will get in your way. You need bring only the items mentioned in the official notice you received; usually everything you need is provided. Do not bring reference books to the exam. They will only confuse those last minutes and be taken away from you when in the test room.
- Arrive somewhat ahead of time – If because of transportation schedules you must get there very early, bring a newspaper or magazine to take your mind off yourself while waiting.
- Locate the examination room – When you have found the proper room, you will be directed to the seat or part of the room where you will sit. Sometimes you are given a sheet of instructions to read while you are waiting. Do not fill out any forms until you are told to do so; just read them and be prepared.
- Relax and prepare to listen to the instructions
- If you have any physical problem that may keep you from doing your best, be sure to tell the test administrator. If you are sick or in poor health, you really cannot do your best on the exam. You can come back and take the test some other time.

VII. AT THE TEST

The day of the test is here and you have the test booklet in your hand. The temptation to get going is very strong. Caution! There is more to success than knowing the right answers. You must know how to identify your papers and understand variations in the type of short-answer question used in this particular examination. Follow these suggestions for maximum results from your efforts:

1) Cooperate with the monitor

The test administrator has a duty to create a situation in which you can be as much at ease as possible. He will give instructions, tell you when to begin, check to see that you are marking your answer sheet correctly, and so on. He is not there to guard you, although he will see that your competitors do not take unfair advantage. He wants to help you do your best.

2) Listen to all instructions

Don't jump the gun! Wait until you understand all directions. In most civil service tests you get more time than you need to answer the questions. So don't be in a hurry. Read each word of instructions until you clearly understand the meaning. Study the examples, listen to all announcements and follow directions. Ask questions if you do not understand what to do.

3) Identify your papers

Civil service exams are usually identified by number only. You will be assigned a number; you must not put your name on your test papers. Be sure to copy your number correctly. Since more than one exam may be given, copy your exact examination title.

4) Plan your time

Unless you are told that a test is a "speed" or "rate of work" test, speed itself is usually not important. Time enough to answer all the questions will be provided, but this does not mean that you have all day. An overall time limit has been set. Divide the total time (in minutes) by the number of questions to determine the approximate time you have for each question.

5) Do not linger over difficult questions

If you come across a difficult question, mark it with a paper clip (useful to have along) and come back to it when you have been through the booklet. One caution if you do this – be sure to skip a number on your answer sheet as well. Check often to be sure that you have not lost your place and that you are marking in the row numbered the same as the question you are answering.

6) Read the questions

Be sure you know what the question asks! Many capable people are unsuccessful because they failed to *read* the questions correctly.

7) Answer all questions

Unless you have been instructed that a penalty will be deducted for incorrect answers, it is better to guess than to omit a question.

8) Speed tests

It is often better NOT to guess on speed tests. It has been found that on timed tests people are tempted to spend the last few seconds before time is called in marking answers at random – without even reading them – in the hope of picking up a few extra points. To discourage this practice, the instructions may warn you that your score will be "corrected" for guessing. That is, a penalty will be applied. The incorrect answers will be deducted from the correct ones, or some other penalty formula will be used.

9) Review your answers

If you finish before time is called, go back to the questions you guessed or omitted to give them further thought. Review other answers if you have time.

10) Return your test materials

If you are ready to leave before others have finished or time is called, take ALL your materials to the monitor and leave quietly. Never take any test material with you. The monitor can discover whose papers are not complete, and taking a test booklet may be grounds for disqualification.

VIII. EXAMINATION TECHNIQUES

1) Read the general instructions carefully. These are usually printed on the first page of the exam booklet. As a rule, these instructions refer to the timing of the examination; the fact that you should not start work until the signal and must stop work at a signal, etc. If there are any *special* instructions, such as a choice of questions to be answered, make sure that you note this instruction carefully.

2) When you are ready to start work on the examination, that is as soon as the signal has been given, read the instructions to each question booklet, underline any key words or phrases, such as *least, best, outline, describe* and the like. In this way you will tend to answer as requested rather than discover on reviewing your paper that you *listed without describing*, that you selected the *worst* choice rather than the *best* choice, etc.

3) If the examination is of the objective or multiple-choice type – that is, each question will also give a series of possible answers: A, B, C or D, and you are called upon to select the best answer and write the letter next to that answer on your answer paper – it is advisable to start answering each question in turn. There may be anywhere from 50 to 100 such questions in the three or four hours allotted and you can see how much time would be taken if you read through all the questions before beginning to answer any. Furthermore, if you come across a question or group of questions which you know would be difficult to answer, it would undoubtedly affect your handling of all the other questions.

4) If the examination is of the essay type and contains but a few questions, it is a moot point as to whether you should read all the questions before starting to answer any one. Of course, if you are given a choice – say five out of seven and the like – then it is essential to read all the questions so you can eliminate the two that are most difficult. If, however, you are asked to answer all the questions, there may be danger in trying to answer the easiest one first because you may find that you will spend too much time on it. The best technique is to answer the first question, then proceed to the second, etc.

5) Time your answers. Before the exam begins, write down the time it started, then add the time allowed for the examination and write down the time it must be completed, then divide the time available somewhat as follows:

- If 3-1/2 hours are allowed, that would be 210 minutes. If you have 80 objective-type questions, that would be an average of 2-1/2 minutes per question. Allow yourself no more than 2 minutes per question, or a total of 160 minutes, which will permit about 50 minutes to review.
- If for the time allotment of 210 minutes there are 7 essay questions to answer, that would average about 30 minutes a question. Give yourself only 25 minutes per question so that you have about 35 minutes to review.

6) The most important instruction is to *read each question* and make sure you know what is wanted. The second most important instruction is to *time yourself properly* so that you answer every question. The third most important instruction is to *answer every question*. Guess if you have to but include something for each question. Remember that you will receive no credit for a blank and will probably receive some credit if you write something in answer to an essay question. If you guess a letter – say "B" for a multiple-choice question – you may have guessed right. If you leave a blank as an answer to a multiple-choice question, the examiners may respect your feelings but it will not add a point to your score. Some exams may penalize you for wrong answers, so in such cases *only*, you may not want to guess unless you have some basis for your answer.

7) Suggestions
   a. Objective-type questions
      1. Examine the question booklet for proper sequence of pages and questions
      2. Read all instructions carefully
      3. Skip any question which seems too difficult; return to it after all other questions have been answered
      4. Apportion your time properly; do not spend too much time on any single question or group of questions
      5. Note and underline key words – *all, most, fewest, least, best, worst, same, opposite,* etc.
      6. Pay particular attention to negatives
      7. Note unusual option, e.g., unduly long, short, complex, different or similar in content to the body of the question
      8. Observe the use of "hedging" words – *probably, may, most likely,* etc.
      9. Make sure that your answer is put next to the same number as the question
      10. Do not second-guess unless you have good reason to believe the second answer is definitely more correct
      11. Cross out original answer if you decide another answer is more accurate; do not erase until you are ready to hand your paper in
      12. Answer all questions; guess unless instructed otherwise
      13. Leave time for review

   b. Essay questions
      1. Read each question carefully
      2. Determine exactly what is wanted. Underline key words or phrases.
      3. Decide on outline or paragraph answer

4. Include many different points and elements unless asked to develop any one or two points or elements
5. Show impartiality by giving pros and cons unless directed to select one side only
6. Make and write down any assumptions you find necessary to answer the questions
7. Watch your English, grammar, punctuation and choice of words
8. Time your answers; don't crowd material

8) Answering the essay question

Most essay questions can be answered by framing the specific response around several key words or ideas. Here are a few such key words or ideas:

M's: manpower, materials, methods, money, management
P's: purpose, program, policy, plan, procedure, practice, problems, pitfalls, personnel, public relations
   a. Six basic steps in handling problems:
      1. Preliminary plan and background development
      2. Collect information, data and facts
      3. Analyze and interpret information, data and facts
      4. Analyze and develop solutions as well as make recommendations
      5. Prepare report and sell recommendations
      6. Install recommendations and follow up effectiveness

   b. Pitfalls to avoid
      1. *Taking things for granted* – A statement of the situation does not necessarily imply that each of the elements is necessarily true; for example, a complaint may be invalid and biased so that all that can be taken for granted is that a complaint has been registered
      2. *Considering only one side of a situation* – Wherever possible, indicate several alternatives and then point out the reasons you selected the best one
      3. *Failing to indicate follow up* – Whenever your answer indicates action on your part, make certain that you will take proper follow-up action to see how successful your recommendations, procedures or actions turn out to be
      4. *Taking too long in answering any single question* – Remember to time your answers properly

IX. AFTER THE TEST

Scoring procedures differ in detail among civil service jurisdictions although the general principles are the same. Whether the papers are hand-scored or graded by machine we have described, they are nearly always graded by number. That is, the person who marks the paper knows only the number – never the name – of the applicant. Not until all the papers have been graded will they be matched with names. If other tests, such as training and experience or oral interview ratings have been given, scores will be combined. Different parts of the examination usually have different weights. For example, the written test might count 60 percent of the final grade, and a rating of training and experience 40 percent. In many jurisdictions, veterans will have a certain number of points added to their grades.

After the final grade has been determined, the names are placed in grade order and an eligible list is established. There are various methods for resolving ties between those who get the same final grade – probably the most common is to place first the name of the person whose application was received first. Job offers are made from the eligible list in the order the names appear on it. You will be notified of your grade and your rank as soon as all these computations have been made. This will be done as rapidly as possible.

People who are found to meet the requirements in the announcement are called "eligibles." Their names are put on a list of eligible candidates. An eligible's chances of getting a job depend on how high he stands on this list and how fast agencies are filling jobs from the list.

When a job is to be filled from a list of eligibles, the agency asks for the names of people on the list of eligibles for that job. When the civil service commission receives this request, it sends to the agency the names of the three people highest on this list. Or, if the job to be filled has specialized requirements, the office sends the agency the names of the top three persons who meet these requirements from the general list.

The appointing officer makes a choice from among the three people whose names were sent to him. If the selected person accepts the appointment, the names of the others are put back on the list to be considered for future openings.

That is the rule in hiring from all kinds of eligible lists, whether they are for typist, carpenter, chemist, or something else. For every vacancy, the appointing officer has his choice of any one of the top three eligibles on the list. This explains why the person whose name is on top of the list sometimes does not get an appointment when some of the persons lower on the list do. If the appointing officer chooses the second or third eligible, the No. 1 eligible does not get a job at once, but stays on the list until he is appointed or the list is terminated.

X. HOW TO PASS THE INTERVIEW TEST

The examination for which you applied requires an oral interview test. You have already taken the written test and you are now being called for the interview test – the final part of the formal examination.

You may think that it is not possible to prepare for an interview test and that there are no procedures to follow during an interview. Our purpose is to point out some things you can do in advance that will help you and some good rules to follow and pitfalls to avoid while you are being interviewed.

What is an interview supposed to test?
The written examination is designed to test the technical knowledge and competence of the candidate; the oral is designed to evaluate intangible qualities, not readily measured otherwise, and to establish a list showing the relative fitness of each candidate – as measured against his competitors – for the position sought. Scoring is not on the basis of "right" and "wrong," but on a sliding scale of values ranging from "not passable" to "outstanding." As a matter of fact, it is possible to achieve a relatively low score without a single "incorrect" answer because of evident weakness in the qualities being measured.

Occasionally, an examination may consist entirely of an oral test – either an individual or a group oral. In such cases, information is sought concerning the technical knowledges and abilities of the candidate, since there has been no written examination for this purpose. More commonly, however, an oral test is used to supplement a written examination.

Who conducts interviews?

The composition of oral boards varies among different jurisdictions. In nearly all, a representative of the personnel department serves as chairman. One of the members of the board may be a representative of the department in which the candidate would work. In some cases, "outside experts" are used, and, frequently, a businessman or some other representative of the general public is asked to serve. Labor and management or other special groups may be represented. The aim is to secure the services of experts in the appropriate field.

However the board is composed, it is a good idea (and not at all improper or unethical) to ascertain in advance of the interview who the members are and what groups they represent. When you are introduced to them, you will have some idea of their backgrounds and interests, and at least you will not stutter and stammer over their names.

What should be done before the interview?

While knowledge about the board members is useful and takes some of the surprise element out of the interview, there is other preparation which is more substantive. It *is* possible to prepare for an oral interview – in several ways:

1) Keep a copy of your application and review it carefully before the interview

This may be the only document before the oral board, and the starting point of the interview. Know what education and experience you have listed there, and the sequence and dates of all of it. Sometimes the board will ask you to review the highlights of your experience for them; you should not have to hem and haw doing it.

2) Study the class specification and the examination announcement

Usually, the oral board has one or both of these to guide them. The qualities, characteristics or knowledges required by the position sought are stated in these documents. They offer valuable clues as to the nature of the oral interview. For example, if the job involves supervisory responsibilities, the announcement will usually indicate that knowledge of modern supervisory methods and the qualifications of the candidate as a supervisor will be tested. If so, you can expect such questions, frequently in the form of a hypothetical situation which you are expected to solve. NEVER go into an oral without knowledge of the duties and responsibilities of the job you seek.

3) Think through each qualification required

Try to visualize the kind of questions you would ask if you were a board member. How well could you answer them? Try especially to appraise your own knowledge and background in each area, *measured against the job sought*, and identify any areas in which you are weak. Be critical and realistic – do not flatter yourself.

4) Do some general reading in areas in which you feel you may be weak

For example, if the job involves supervision and your past experience has NOT, some general reading in supervisory methods and practices, particularly in the field of human relations, might be useful. Do NOT study agency procedures or detailed manuals. The oral board will be testing your understanding and capacity, not your memory.

5) Get a good night's sleep and watch your general health and mental attitude

You will want a clear head at the interview. Take care of a cold or any other minor ailment, and of course, no hangovers.

What should be done on the day of the interview?

Now comes the day of the interview itself. Give yourself plenty of time to get there. Plan to arrive somewhat ahead of the scheduled time, particularly if your appointment is in the fore part of the day. If a previous candidate fails to appear, the board might be ready for you a bit early. By early afternoon an oral board is almost invariably behind schedule if there are many candidates, and you may have to wait. Take along a book or magazine to read, or your application to review, but leave any extraneous material in the waiting room when you go in for your interview. In any event, relax and compose yourself.

The matter of dress is important. The board is forming impressions about you – from your experience, your manners, your attitude, and your appearance. Give your personal appearance careful attention. Dress your best, but not your flashiest. Choose conservative, appropriate clothing, and be sure it is immaculate. This is a business interview, and your appearance should indicate that you regard it as such. Besides, being well groomed and properly dressed will help boost your confidence.

Sooner or later, someone will call your name and escort you into the interview room. *This is it.* From here on you are on your own. It is too late for any more preparation. But remember, you asked for this opportunity to prove your fitness, and you are here because your request was granted.

What happens when you go in?

The usual sequence of events will be as follows: The clerk (who is often the board stenographer) will introduce you to the chairman of the oral board, who will introduce you to the other members of the board. Acknowledge the introductions before you sit down. Do not be surprised if you find a microphone facing you or a stenotypist sitting by. Oral interviews are usually recorded in the event of an appeal or other review.

Usually the chairman of the board will open the interview by reviewing the highlights of your education and work experience from your application – primarily for the benefit of the other members of the board, as well as to get the material into the record. Do not interrupt or comment unless there is an error or significant misinterpretation; if that is the case, do not hesitate. But do not quibble about insignificant matters. Also, he will usually ask you some question about your education, experience or your present job – partly to get you to start talking and to establish the interviewing "rapport." He may start the actual questioning, or turn it over to one of the other members. Frequently, each member undertakes the questioning on a particular area, one in which he is perhaps most competent, so you can expect each member to participate in the examination. Because time is limited, you may also expect some rather abrupt switches in the direction the questioning takes, so do not be upset by it. Normally, a board member will not pursue a single line of questioning unless he discovers a particular strength or weakness.

After each member has participated, the chairman will usually ask whether any member has any further questions, then will ask you if you have anything you wish to add. Unless you are expecting this question, it may floor you. Worse, it may start you off on an extended, extemporaneous speech. The board is not usually seeking more information. The question is principally to offer you a last opportunity to present further qualifications or to indicate that you have nothing to add. So, if you feel that a significant qualification or characteristic has been overlooked, it is proper to point it out in a sentence or so. Do not compliment the board on the thoroughness of their examination – they have been sketchy, and you know it. If you wish, merely say, "No thank you, I have nothing further to add." This is a point where you can "talk yourself out" of a good impression or fail to present an important bit of information. Remember, *you close the interview yourself.*

The chairman will then say, "That is all, Mr. _____, thank you." Do not be startled; the interview is over, and quicker than you think. Thank him, gather your belongings and take your leave. Save your sigh of relief for the other side of the door.

How to put your best foot forward

Throughout this entire process, you may feel that the board individually and collectively is trying to pierce your defenses, seek out your hidden weaknesses and embarrass and confuse you. Actually, this is not true. They are obliged to make an appraisal of your qualifications for the job you are seeking, and they want to see you in your best light. Remember, they must interview all candidates and a non-cooperative candidate may become a failure in spite of their best efforts to bring out his qualifications. Here are 15 suggestions that will help you:

1) Be natural – Keep your attitude confident, not cocky

If you are not confident that you can do the job, do not expect the board to be. Do not apologize for your weaknesses, try to bring out your strong points. The board is interested in a positive, not negative, presentation. Cockiness will antagonize any board member and make him wonder if you are covering up a weakness by a false show of strength.

2) Get comfortable, but don't lounge or sprawl

Sit erectly but not stiffly. A careless posture may lead the board to conclude that you are careless in other things, or at least that you are not impressed by the importance of the occasion. Either conclusion is natural, even if incorrect. Do not fuss with your clothing, a pencil or an ashtray. Your hands may occasionally be useful to emphasize a point; do not let them become a point of distraction.

3) Do not wisecrack or make small talk

This is a serious situation, and your attitude should show that you consider it as such. Further, the time of the board is limited – they do not want to waste it, and neither should you.

4) Do not exaggerate your experience or abilities

In the first place, from information in the application or other interviews and sources, the board may know more about you than you think. Secondly, you probably will not get away with it. An experienced board is rather adept at spotting such a situation, so do not take the chance.

5) If you know a board member, do not make a point of it, yet do not hide it

Certainly you are not fooling him, and probably not the other members of the board. Do not try to take advantage of your acquaintanceship – it will probably do you little good.

6) Do not dominate the interview

Let the board do that. They will give you the clues – do not assume that you have to do all the talking. Realize that the board has a number of questions to ask you, and do not try to take up all the interview time by showing off your extensive knowledge of the answer to the first one.

7) Be attentive

You only have 20 minutes or so, and you should keep your attention at its sharpest throughout. When a member is addressing a problem or question to you, give him your undivided attention. Address your reply principally to him, but do not exclude the other board members.

8) Do not interrupt

A board member may be stating a problem for you to analyze. He will ask you a question when the time comes. Let him state the problem, and wait for the question.

9) Make sure you understand the question

Do not try to answer until you are sure what the question is. If it is not clear, restate it in your own words or ask the board member to clarify it for you. However, do not haggle about minor elements.

10) Reply promptly but not hastily

A common entry on oral board rating sheets is "candidate responded readily," or "candidate hesitated in replies." Respond as promptly and quickly as you can, but do not jump to a hasty, ill-considered answer.

11) Do not be peremptory in your answers

A brief answer is proper – but do not fire your answer back. That is a losing game from your point of view. The board member can probably ask questions much faster than you can answer them.

12) Do not try to create the answer you think the board member wants

He is interested in what kind of mind you have and how it works – not in playing games. Furthermore, he can usually spot this practice and will actually grade you down on it.

13) Do not switch sides in your reply merely to agree with a board member

Frequently, a member will take a contrary position merely to draw you out and to see if you are willing and able to defend your point of view. Do not start a debate, yet do not surrender a good position. If a position is worth taking, it is worth defending.

14) Do not be afraid to admit an error in judgment if you are shown to be wrong

The board knows that you are forced to reply without any opportunity for careful consideration. Your answer may be demonstrably wrong. If so, admit it and get on with the interview.

15) Do not dwell at length on your present job

The opening question may relate to your present assignment. Answer the question but do not go into an extended discussion. You are being examined for a *new* job, not your present one. As a matter of fact, try to phrase ALL your answers in terms of the job for which you are being examined.

Basis of Rating

Probably you will forget most of these "do's" and "don'ts" when you walk into the oral interview room. Even remembering them all will not ensure you a passing grade. Perhaps you did not have the qualifications in the first place. But remembering them will help you to put your best foot forward, without treading on the toes of the board members.

Rumor and popular opinion to the contrary notwithstanding, an oral board wants you to make the best appearance possible. They know you are under pressure – but they also want to see how you respond to it as a guide to what your reaction would be under the pressures of the job you seek. They will be influenced by the degree of poise you display, the personal traits you show and the manner in which you respond.

ABOUT THIS BOOK

This book contains tests divided into Examination Sections. Go through each test, answering every question in the margin. At the end of each test look at the answer key and check your answers. On the ones you got wrong, look at the right answer choice and learn. Do not fill in the answers first. Do not memorize the questions and answers, but understand the answer and principles involved. On your test, the questions will likely be different from the samples. Questions are changed and new ones added. If you understand these past questions you should have success with any changes that arise. Tests may consist of several types of questions. We have additional books on each subject should more study be advisable or necessary for you. Finally, the more you study, the better prepared you will be. This book is intended to be the last thing you study before you walk into the examination room. Prior study of relevant texts is also recommended. NLC publishes some of these in our Fundamental Series. Knowledge and good sense are important factors in passing your exam. Good luck also helps. So now study this Passbook, absorb the material contained within and take that knowledge into the examination. Then do your best to pass that exam.

EXAMINATION SECTION

ARITHMETIC COMPUTATION

EXAMINATION SECTION

TEST 1

The following sample questions show types of questions that will be used in the written test. They also show how the answers to the questions are to be recorded. Read the directions for each set of questions, and answer them. Record your answers on the Sample Answer Sheets provided on each page of this section. Then compare your answers with those given in the *CORRECT ANSWERS* to Sample Questions on the same page.

Solve each problem and see which of the suggested answers A, B, C, or D is correct. Darken the space on the Sample Answer Sheet corresponding to the correct answer. If your answer does not exactly agree with any of the first four suggested answers, darken space E.

ADDITION
Questions 1-5.

1. Add: 129
        958
        787
        436

   A. 3310   B. 2308   C. 2312   D. 2310   E. none of these

2.. Add: 9,497
         6,364
         4,269
         9,785

   A 28,915   B. 29,917   C. 29,915   D. 29,925   E. none of these

3. Add: 67,856
        22,851
        44,238
        97,156

   A. 231,101   B. 211,101   C. 212,101   D. 232,111   E. none of these

4. Add: 23
          468
            7
        9,045
           76
            8

   A. 9,627   B. 9,527   C. 9,617   D. 8,627   E none of these

5. Add: 87,651
43,212
76,543
34,564
91,205
34,566

    A. 367,641   B. 367,741   C. 368,741   D. 368,641   E. none of these

---

KEY (CORRECT ANSWERS)

1. D
2. C
3. E
4. A
5. B

SOLUTIONS TO PROBLEMS

1. 129 + 958 + 787 + 436 = 2310
2. 9497 + 6364 + 4269 + 9785 = 29,915
3. 67,856 + 22,851 + 44,238 + 97,156 = 232,141
4. 23 + 468 + 7 + 9045 + 76 +8 = 9627
5. 87,651 + 43,212 + 76,543 + 34,564 + 91,205 + 34,566 = 367,741

———————

TEST 2

SUBTRACTION
Question 1-5.

1. Subtract: 390
              -169
   A. 217   B. 218   C. 219   D. 220   E. none of these

2. Subtract: 639
              -378
   A. 263   B. 262   C. 261   D. 260   E. none of these

3. Subtract: 709
              - 594
   A. 115   B. 114   C. 113   D. 112   E. none of these

4. Subtract: 3,457
              -2,498
   A. 955   B. 956   C. 957   D. 958   E. none of these

5. Subtract: 8,752
              -4,658
   A. 4074   B. 4084   C. 4194   D. 4094   E. none of these

———

KEY (CORRECT ANSWERS)

1. E
2. C
3. A
4. E
5. D

———

SOLUTIONS TO PROBLEMS

1. 390 - 169 = 221
2. 639 - 378 = 261
3. 709 - 594 = 115
4. 3457 - 2498 = 959
5. 8752 - 4658 = 4094

———————

TEST 3

MULTIPLICATION
Questions 1-5.

1. Multiply: 36
              x5

   A. 190   B. 160   C. 180   D. 365   E. none of these

2. Multiply: 86
              x6

   A. 486   B. 506   C. 536   D. 866   E. none of these

3. Multiply: 40
              x4

   A. 160   B. 440   C. 164   D. 180   E. none of these

4. Multiply: 95
              x2

   A. 952   B. 180   C. 190   D. 195   E. none of these

5. Multiply: 52
              x7

   A. 347   B. 346   C. 527   D. 364   E. none of these

———

KEY (CORRECT ANSWERS)

1. C
2. E
3. A
4. C
5. D

———

2 (#3)

SOLUTIONS TO PROBLEMS

1.   (36)(5) = 180
2.   (86)(6) = 516
3.   (40)(4) = 160
4.   (95)(2) = 190
5.   (52)(7) = 364

———————

TEST 4

<u>DIVISION</u>
Questions 1-5.

1. Divide: $546 \div 9$
   A. 60   B. 60 3/9   C. 60 6/9   D. 61   E. none of these

2. Divide: $\sqrt[8]{247}$
   A. 30   B. 30 1/8   C. 30 3/8   D. 30 5/8   E. none of these

3. Divide: $\dfrac{289}{4}$
   A. 72   B. 72 1/8   C. 72 3/8   D. 72 ½   E. none of these

4. Divide: $363 \div 4$
   A. 91   B. 92   C. 90 ¼   D. 90 ¾   E. none of these

5. Divide: $\dfrac{304}{4}$
   A. 75 1/4   B. 76   C. 75 ¼   D. 76 ¼   E. none of these

KEY (CORRECT ANSWERS)

1. C
2. E
3. E
4. D
5. B

SOLUTIONS TO PROBLEMS

1.   546 ÷ 9 = 60 6/9 or 60 2/3
2.   247 ÷ 8 = 30.875 = 30 7/8
3.   289 ÷ 4 = 72.25 = 72 1/4
4.   363 ÷ 4 = 90.75 = 90 3/4
5.   304 ÷ 4 = 76

ARITHMETIC

EXAMINATION SECTION
TEST 1

DIRECTIONS: Each question or incomplete statement is followed by several suggested answers or completions. Select the one that BEST answers the question or completes the statement. *PRINT THE LETTER OF THE CORRECT ANSWER IN THE SPACE AT THE RIGHT.*

1. From 30983 subtract 29998. The answer should be

    A. 985   B. 995   C. 1005   D. 1015

1.____

2. From $2537.75 subtract $1764.28. The answer should be

    A. $763.58   B. $773.47   C. $774.48   D. $873.58

2.____

3. From 254211 subtract 76348. The answer should be

    A. 177863   B. 177963   C. 187963   D. 188973

3.____

4. Divide 4025 by 35. The answer should be

    A. 105   B. 109   C. 115   D. 125

4.____

5. Multiply 0.35 by 2764. The answer should be

    A. 997.50   B. 967.40   C. 957.40   D. 834.40

5.____

6. Multiply 1367 by 0.50. The answer should be

    A. 6.8350   B. 68.350   C. 683.50   D. 6835.0

6.____

7. Multiply 841 by 0.01. The answer should be

    A. 0.841   B. 8.41   C. 84.1   D. 841

7.____

8. Multiply 1962 by 25. The answer should be

    A. 47740   B. 48460   C. 48950   D. 49050

8.____

9. Multiply 905 by 0.05. The answer should be

    A. 452.5   B. 45.25   C. 4.525   D. 0.4525

9.____

10. Multiply 8.93 by 4.7. The answer should be

    A. 41.971   B. 40.871   C. 4.1971   D. 4.0871

10.____

11. Multiply 25 by 763. The answer should be

    A. 18075   B. 18875   C. 19075   D. 20965

11.____

12. Multiply 2530 by 0.10. The answer should be

    A. 2.5300   B. 25.300   C. 253.00   D. 2530.0

12.____

13. Multiply 3053 by 0.25. The answer should be 13._____

    A. 76.325   B. 86.315   C. 763.25   D. 863.15

14. Multiply 6204 by 0.35. The answer should be 14._____

    A. 2282.40   B. 2171.40   C. 228.24   D. 217.14

15. Multiply $.35 by 7619. The answer should be 15._____

    A. $2324.75   B. $2565.65   C. $2666.65   D. $2756.75

16. Multiply 6513 by 45. The answer should be 16._____

    A. 293185   B. 293085   C. 292185   D. 270975

17. Multiply 3579 by 70. The answer should be 17._____

    A. 25053.0   B. 240530   C. 250530   D. 259530

18. A class had an average of 24 words correct on a spelling test. The class average on this spelling test was 80%.
The AVERAGE number of words missed on this test was 18._____

    A. 2   B. 4   C. 6   D. 8

19. In which one of the following is 24 renamed as a product of primes? 19._____

    A. 2 x 6 x 2   B. 8 x 3 x 1
    C. 2 x 2 x 3 x 2   D. 3 x 4 x 2

Questions 20-23.

DIRECTIONS: In answering Questions 20 through 23, perform the indicated operation. Select the BEST answer from the choices below.

20. Add: 7068
           2807
           9434
           6179 20._____

    A. 26,488   B. 24,588   C. 25,488   D. 25,478

21. Divide: $75\sqrt{45555}$ 21._____

    A. 674   B. 607.4   C. 6074   D. 60.74

22. Multiply: 907
             x806 22._____

    A. 73,142   B. 13,202   C. 721,042   D. 731,042

23. Subtract: 60085
            -47194 23._____

    A. 12,891   B. 13,891   C. 12,991   D. 12,871

24. A librarian reported that 1/5% of all books taken out last school year had not been returned.
   If 85,000 books were borrowed from the library, how many were not returned?

   A. 170   B. 425   C. 1,700   D. 4,250

24.____

25. At 40 miles per hour, how many minutes would it take to travel 12 miles?

   A. 30   B. 18   C. 15   D. 20

25.____

KEY (CORRECT ANSWERS)

1.	A	11.	C
2.	B	12.	C
3.	A	13.	C
4.	C	14.	B
5.	B	15.	C
6.	C	16.	B
7.	B	17.	C
8.	D	18.	C
9.	B	19.	C
10.	A	20.	C

21.	B
22.	D
23.	A
24.	A
25.	B

13

SOLUTIONS TO PROBLEMS

1. 30,983 - 29,998 = 985

2. $2537.75 - $1764.28 = $773.47

3. 254,211 - 76,348 = 177,863

4. 4025 ÷ 35 = 115

5. (.35)(2764) = 967.4

6. (1367)(.50) = 683.5

7. (841)(.01) = 8.41

8. (1962)(25) = 49,050

9. (905)(.05) = 45.25

10. (8.93)(4.7) = 41.971

11. (25)(763) = 19,075

12. (2530)(.10) = 253

13. (3053)(.25) = 763.25

14. (6204)(.35) = 2171.4

15. ($.35)(7619) = $2666.65

16. (6513)(45) = 293,085

17. (3579)(70) = 250,530

18. 24 ÷ .80 = 30. Then, 30 - 24 = 6 words

19. 24 = 2 x 2 x 3 x 2, where each number is a prime.

20. 7068 ÷ 2807 + 9434 + 6179 = 25,488

21. 45,555 ÷ 75 = 607.4

22. (907)(806) = 731,042

23. 60,085 - 47,194 = 12,891

24. (1/5%)(85,000) = (.002)(85,000) = 170 books

25. Let x = number of minutes. Then, $\frac{40}{60} = \frac{12}{x}$. Solving, x = 18

———

TEST 2

DIRECTIONS: Each question or incomplete statement is followed by several **suggested** answers or completions. Select the one that BEST answers the question or completes the statement. *PRINT THE LETTER OF THE CORRECT ANSWER IN THE SPACE AT THE RIGHT.*

1. The sum of 57901 + 34762 is

    A. 81663　　　B. 82663　　　C. 91663　　　D. 92663

    1.____

2. The sum of 559 + 448 + 362 + 662 is

    A. 2121　　　B. 2031　　　C. 2021　　　D. 1931

    2.____

3. The sum of 36153 + 28624 + 81379 is

    A. 136156　　　B. 146046　　　C. 146146　　　D. 146156

    3.____

4. The sum of 742 + 9197 + 8972 is

    A. 19901　　　B. 18911　　　C. 18801　　　D. 17921

    4.____

5. The sum of 7989 + 8759 + 2726 is

    A. 18455　　　B. 18475　　　C. 19464　　　D. 19474

    5.____

6. The sum of $111.55 + $95.05 + $38.80 is

    A. $234.40　　　B. $235.30　　　C. $245.40　　　D. $254.50

    6.____

7. The sum of 1302 + 46187 + 92610 + 4522 is

    A. 144621　　　B. 143511　　　C. 134621　　　D. 134521

    7.____

8. The sum of 47953 + 58041 + 63022 + 22333 is

    A. 170248　　　B. 181349　　　C. 191349　　　D. 200359

    8.____

9. The sum of 76563 + 43693 + 38521 + 50987 + 72723 is

    A. 271378　　　B. 282386　　　C. 282487　　　D. 292597

    9.____

10. The sum of 85923 + 97211 + 11333 + 4412 + 22533 is

    A. 209302　　　B. 212422　　　C. 221412　　　D. 221533

    10.____

11. The sum of 4299 + 54163 + 89765 + 1012 + 38962 is

    A. 188201　　　B. 188300　　　C. 188301　　　D. 189311

    11.____

12. The sum of 48526 + 709 + 11534 + 80432 + 6096 is

    A. 135177　　　B. 139297　　　C. 147297　　　D. 149197

    12.____

13. The sum of $407.62 + $109.01 + $68.44 + $378.68 is

    A. $963.75　　　B. $964.85　　　C. $973.65　　　D. $974.85

    13.____

14. From 40614 subtract 4697. The answer should be   14.____

    A.   35917   B.   35927   C.   36023   D.   36027

15. From 81773 subtract 5717. The answer should be   15.____

    A.   75964   B.   76056   C.   76066   D.   76956

16. From $1755.35 subtract $1201.75. The answer should be   16.____

    A. $542.50   B. $544.50   C. $553.60   D. $554.60

17. From $2402.10 subtract $998.85. The answer should be   17.____

    A. $1514.35   B. $1504.25   C. $1413.25   D. $1403.25

18. Add: 12 1/2   18.____

           2 1/2

          3 1/2

    A. 17   B. 17 1/4   C. 17 3/4   D. 18

19. Subtract: 150   19.____

          -80

    A. 70   B. 80   C. 130   D. 150

20. After cleaning up some lots in the city dump, five cleanup crews loaded the following   20.____
amounts of garbage on trucks:
        Crew No. 1 loaded 2 1/4 tons
        Crew No. 2 loaded 3 tons
        Crew No. 3 loaded 1 1/4 tons
        Crew No. 4 loaded 2 1/4tons
        Crew No. 5 loaded 1/2 ton.
The TOTAL number of tons of garbage loaded was

    A. 8 1/4   B. 8 3/4   C. 9   D. 9 1/4

21. Subtract: 17 3/4   21.____

        -7 1/4

    A. 7 1/2   B. 10 1/2   C. 14 1/4   D. 17 3/4

22. Yesterday, Tom and Bill each received 10 leaflets about rat control. They were supposed   22.____
to distribute one leaflet to each supermarket in the neighborhood. When the day was
over, Tom had 8 leaflets left. Bill had no leaflets left.
How many supermarkets got leaflets yesterday?

    A. 8   B. 10   C. 12   D. 18

23. What is 2/3 of 1 1/8?   23.____

    A. 1 11/16   B. 3/4   C. 3/8   D. 4 1/3

24. A farmer bought a load of 120 bushels of corn.   24.____
After he fed 45 bushels to his hogs, what fraction of his supply remained?

    A. 5/8   B. 3/5   C. 3/8   D. 4/7

25. In the numeral 3,159,217, the 2 is in the _____ column.   25.____

    A.   hundreds   B.   units   C.   thousands   D.   tens

KEY (CORRECT ANSWERS)

1.	D		11.	A
2.	B		12.	C
3.	D		13.	A
4.	B		14.	A
5.	D		15.	B
6.	C		16.	C
7.	A		17.	D
8.	C		18.	D
9.	C		19.	A
10.	C		20.	D

21.	B
22.	C
23.	B
24.	A
25.	A

SOLUTIONS TO PROBLEMS

1. $57{,}901 + 34{,}762 = 92{,}663$

2. $559 + 448 + 362 + 662 = 2031$

3. $36{,}153 + 28{,}624 + 81{,}379 = 146{,}156$

4. $742 + 9197 + 8972 = 18{,}911$

5. $7989 + 8759 + 2726 = 19{,}474$

6. $\$111.55 + \$95.05 + \$38.80 = \$245.40$

7. $1302 + 46{,}187 + 92{,}610 + 4522 = 144{,}621$

8. $47{,}953 + 58{,}041 + 63{,}022 + 22{,}333 = 191{,}349$

9. $76{,}563 + 45{,}693 + 38{,}521 + 50{,}987 + 72{,}723 = 282{,}487$

10. $85{,}923 + 97{,}211 + 11{,}333 + 4412 + 22{,}533 = 221{,}412$

11. $4299 + 54{,}163 + 89{,}765 + 1012 + 38{,}962 = 188{,}201$

12. $48{,}526 + 709 + 11{,}534 + 80{,}432 + 6096 = 147{,}297$

13. $\$407.62 + \$109.01 + \$68.44 + \$378.68 = \$963.75$

14. $40{,}614 - 4697 = 35{,}917$

15. $81{,}773 - 5717 = 76{,}056$

16. $\$1755.35 - \$1201.75 = \$553.60$

17. $\$2402.10 - \$998.85 = \$1403.25$

18. $12\ 1/2 + 2\ 1/4 + 3\ 1/4 = 17\ 4/4 = 18$

19. $150 - 80 = 70$

20. $2\ 1/4 + 3 + 1\ 1/4 + 2\ 1/4 + 1/2 = 8\ 5/4 = 9\ 1/4$ tons

21. $17\ 3/4 - 7\ 1/4 = 10\ 2/4 = 10\ 1/2$

22. $10 + 10 - 8 - 0 = 12$ supermarkets

23. $\left(\dfrac{2}{3}\right)\left(1\dfrac{1}{8}\right) = \left(\dfrac{2}{3}\right)\left(\dfrac{9}{8}\right) = \dfrac{18}{24} = \dfrac{3}{4}$

24. $120 - 45 = 75$. Then, $\dfrac{75}{120} = \dfrac{5}{8}$

25. The number 2 is in the hundreds column of 3,159,217

TEST 3

DIRECTIONS: Each question or incomplete statement is followed by several suggested answers or completions. Select the one that BEST answers the question or completes the statement. *PRINT THE LETTER OF THE CORRECT ANSWER IN THE SPACE AT THE RIGHT.*

1. The distance covered in three minutes by a subway train traveling at 30 mph is _____ mile(s).   1.____

   A. 3   B. 2   C. 1 1/2   D. 1

2. A crate contains 3 pieces of equipment weighing 73, 84, and 47 pounds, respectively. The empty crate weighs 16 pounds.   2.____
   If the crate is lifted by 4 trackmen, each trackman lifting one corner of the crate, the AVERAGE number of pounds lifted by each of the trackmen is

   A. 68   B. 61   C. 55   D. 51

3. The weight per foot of a length of square-bar 4" x 4" in cross-section, as compared with one 2" x 2" in cross-section, is _____ as much.   3.____

   A. twice   B. 2 1/2 times
   C. 3 times   D. 4 times

4. An order for 360 feet of 2" x 8" lumber is shipped in 20-foot lengths.   4.____
   The MAXIMUM number of 9-foot pieces that can be cut from this shipment is

   A. 54   B. 40   C. 36   D. 18

5. If a trackman gets $10.40 per hour and time and one-half for working over 40 hours, his gross salary for a week in which he worked 44 hours should be   5.____

   A. $457.60   B. $478.40   C. $499.20   D. $514.80

6. If a section of ballast 6'-0" wide, 8'-0" long, and 2'-6" deep is excavated, the amount of ballast removed is _____ cu. feet.   6.____

   A. 96   B. 104   C. 120   D. 144

7. The sum of 7'2 3/4", 0'-2 7/8", 3'-0", 4'-6 3/8", and 1'-9 1/4" is   7.____

   A. 16'-8 1/4"   B. 16'-8 3/4"   C. 16'-9 1/4"   D. 16' -9 3/4"

8. The sum of 3 1/16", 4 1/4", 2 5/8", and 5 7/16" is   8.____

   A. 15 3/16"   B. 15 1/4"   C. 15 3/8"   D. 15 1/2"

9. Add: $51.79, $29.39, and $8.98.   9.____
   The CORRECT answer is

   A. $78.97   B. $88.96   C. $89.06   D. $90.16

10. Add: $72.07 and $31.54. Then subtract $25.75.   10.____
    The CORRECT answer is

    A. $77.86   B. $82.14   C. $88.96   D. $129.36

11. Start with $82.47. Then subtract $25.50, $4.75, and 35¢.
The CORRECT answer is   11.____

    A. $30.60   B. $51.87   C. $52.22   D. $65.25

12. Add: $19.35 and $37.75. Then subtract $9.90 and $19.80.
The CORRECT answer is   12.____

    A. $27.40   B. $37.00   C. $37.30   D. $47.20

13. Add: $153
           114
           210
       +186   13.____

    A. $657   B. $663   C. $713   D. $757

14. Add: $64.91
         13.53
         19.27
         20.00
       +72.84   14.____

    A. $170.25   B. $178.35   C. $180.45   D. $190.55

15. Add: 1963
        1742
     +2497   15.____

    A. 6202   B. 6022   C. 5212   D. 5102

16. Add: 206
        709
     1342
     +2076   16.____

    A. 3432   B. 3443   C. 4312   D. 4333

17. Subtract: $190.76
         -    .99   17.____

    A. $189.97   B. $189.87   C. $189.77   D. $189.67

18. From 99876 subtract 85397. The answer should be   18.____

    A. 14589   B. 14521   C. 14479   D. 13589

19. From $876.51 subtract $92.89. The answer should be   19.____

    A. $773.52   B. $774.72   C. $783.62   D. $784.72

20. From 70935 subtract 49489. The answer should be   20.____

    A. 20436   B. 21446   C. 21536   D. 21546

21. From $391.55 subtract $273.45. The answer should be   21._____

   A. $118.10   B. $128.20   C. $178.10   D. $218.20

22. When 119 is subtracted from the sum of 2016 + 1634, the answer is   22._____

   A.   2460   B.   3531   C.   3650   D.   3769

23. Multiply 35 x 65 x 15. The answer should be   23._____

   A.   2275   B.   24265   C.   31145   D.   34125

24. Multiply: 4.06   24._____
             x.031

   A.   1.2586   B.   .12586   C.   .02586   D.   .1786

25. When 65 is added to the result of 14 multiplied by 13, the answer is   25._____

   A.   92   B.   182   C.   247   D.   16055

KEY (CORRECT ANSWERS)

1.	C	11.	B
2.	C	12.	A
3.	D	13.	B
4.	C	14.	D
5.	B	15.	A
6.	C	16.	D
7.	C	17.	C
8.	C	18.	C
9.	D	19.	C
10.	A	20.	B

21.	A
22.	B
23.	D
24.	B
25.	C

SOLUTIONS TO PROBLEMS

1. Let x = distance. Then, $\dfrac{30}{60} = \dfrac{x}{3}$ Solving, x = 1 1/2 miles

2. (73 + 84 + 47 + 16) ÷ 4 = 55 pounds

3. (4 x 4) ÷ (2 x 2) = a ratio of 4 to 1.

4. 20 ÷ 9 = 2 2/9 , rounded down to 2 pieces. Then, (360 ÷ 20)(2) = 36

5. Salary =($10.40)(40) + ($15.60)(4) = $478.40

6. (6)(8)(2 1/2) = 120 cu.ft.

7. $7'2\dfrac{3}{4}" + 0'2\dfrac{7}{8}" + 3'0" + 4'6\dfrac{3}{8}" + 1'9\dfrac{1}{4}" = 15'19\dfrac{18}{8}" = 15'21\dfrac{1}{4}" = 16'9\dfrac{1}{4}"$

8. $3\dfrac{1}{16}" + 4\dfrac{1}{4}" + 2\dfrac{5}{8}" + 5\dfrac{7}{16}" = 14\dfrac{22}{16}" = 15\dfrac{3}{8}"$

9. $51.79 + $29.39 + $8.98 = $90.16

10. $72.07 + $31.54 = $103.61. Then, $103.61 - $25.75 = $77.86

11. $82.47 - $25.50 - $4.75 - $0.35 = $51.87

12. $19.35 + $37.75 = $57.10. Then, $57.10 - $9.90 - $19.80 = $27.40

13. $153 + $114 + $210 + $186 = $663

14. $64.91 + $13.53 + $19.27 + $20.00 + $72.84 = $190.55

15. 1963 + 1742 + 2497 = 6202

16. 206 + 709 + 1342 + 2076 = 4333

17. $190.76 - .99 = $189.77

18. 99,876 - 85,397 = 14,479

19. $876.51 - $92.89 = $783.62

20. 70,935 - 49,489 = 21,446

21. $391.55 - $273.45 = $118.10

22. (2016 + 1634) - 119 = 3650 - 119 = 3531

23. $(35)(65)(15) = 34{,}125$

24. $(4.06)(.031) = .12586$

25. $65 + (14)(13) = 65 + 182 = 247$

———————

ARITHMETIC
EXAMINATION SECTION

DIRECTIONS: Each question or incomplete statement is followed by several suggested answers or completions. Select the one that BEST answers the question or completes the statement. *PRINT THE LETTER OF THE CORRECT ANSWER IN THE SPACE AT THE RIGHT.*

1. The sum of 53632 + 27403 + 98765 + 75424 is   1.____
    A. 19214   B. 215214   C. 235224   D. 255224

2. The sum of 76342 + 49050 + 21206 + 59989 is   2.____
    A. 196586   B. 206087   C. 206587   D. 234487

3. The sum of $452.13 + $963.45 + $621.25 is   3.____
    A. $1936.83   B. $2036.83   C. $2095.73   D. $2135.73

4. The sum of 36392 + 42156 + 98765 is   4.____
    A. 167214   B. 177203   C. 177313   D. 178213

5. The sum of 40125 + 87123 + 24689 is   5.____
    A. 141827   B. 151827   C. 151937   D. 161947

6. The sum of 2379 + 4015 + 6521 + 9986 is   6.____
    A. 22901   B. 22819   C. 21801   D. 21791

7. From 50962 subtract 36197.
The answer should be   7.____
    A. 14675   B. 14765   C. 14865   D. 24765

8. From 90000 subtract 31928.
The answer should be   8.____
    A. 58072   B. 59062   C. 68172   D. 69182

9. From 63764 subtract 21548.
The answer should be   9.____
    A. 42216   B. 43122   C. 45126   D. 85312

10. From $9605.13 subtract $2715.96.
The answer should be   10.____
    A. $12,321.09   B. $8,690.16   C. $6,990.07   D. $6,889.17

11. From 76421 subtract 73101.
The answer should be   11.____
    A. 3642   B. 3540   C. 3320   D. 3242

12. From $8.25 subtract $6.50.
    The answer should be

    A. $1.25   B. $1.50   C. $1.75   D. $2.25

                                                12.____

13. Multiply 563 by 0.50.
    The answer should be

    A. 281.50   B. 28.15   C. 2.815   D. 0.2815

13.____

14. Multiply 0.35 by 1045.
    The answer should be

    A. 0.36575   B. 3.6575   C. 36.575   D. 365.75

14.____

15. Multiply 25 by 2513.
    The answer should be

    A. 62825   B. 62725   C. 60825   D. 52825

15.____

16. Multiply 423 by 0.01.
    The answer should be

    A. 0.0423   B. 0.423   C. 4.23   D. 42.3

16.____

17. Multiply 6.70 by 3.2.
    The answer should be

    A. 2.1440   B. 21.440   C. 214.40   D. 2144.0

17.____

18. Multiply 630 by 517.
    The answer should be

    A. 325,710   B. 345,720   C. 362,425   D. 385,660

18.____

19. Multiply 35 by 846.
    The answer should be

    A. 4050   B. 9450   C. 18740   D. 29610

19.____

20. Multiply 823 by 0.05.
    The answer should be

    A. 0.4115   B. 4.115   C. 41.15   D. 411.50

20.____

21. Multiply 1690 by 0.10.
    The answer should be

    A. 0.169   B. 1.69   C. 16.90   D. 169.0

21.____

22. Divide 2765 by 35.
    The answer should be

    A. 71   B. 79   C. 87   D. 93

22.____

23. From $18.55 subtract $6.80.
    The answer should be

    A. $9.75   B. $10.95   C. $11.75   D. $25.35

23.____

24. The sum of 2.75 + 4.50 + 3.60 is   24._____

    A. 9.75   B. 10.85   C. 11.15   D. 11.95

25. The sum of 9.63 + 11.21 + 17.25 is   25._____

    A. 36.09   B. 38.09   C. 39.92   D. 41.22

26. The sum of 112.0 + 16.9 + 3.84 is   26._____

    A. 129.3   B. 132.74   C. 136.48   D. 167.3

27. When 65 is added to the result of 14 multiplied by 13, the answer is   27._____

    A. 92   B. 182   C. 247   D. 16055

28. From $391.55 subtract $273.45.   28._____
The answer should be

    A. $118.10   B. $128.20   C. $178.10   D. $218.20

29. When 119 is subtracted from the sum of 2016 + 1634, the answer is   29._____

    A. 2460   B. 3531   C. 3650   D. 3769

30. What is $367.20 + $510.00 + $402.80?   30._____

    A. $1,276.90   B. $1,277.90   C. $1,279.00   D. $1,280.00

31. Multiply 35 x 65 x 15.   31._____
The answer should be

    A. 2275   B. 24265   C. 31145   D. 34125

32. Multiply 40 x 65 x 10.   32._____
The answer should be

    A. 26000   B. 28000   C. 25200   D. 22300

33. The total amount of money represented by 43 half-dollars, 26 quarters, and 71 dimes is   33._____

    A. $28.00   B. $35.10   C. $44.30   D. $56.60

34. The total amount of money represented by 132 quarters, 97 dimes, and 220 nickels is   34._____

    A. $43.70   B. $44.20   C. $52.90   D. $53.70

35. The total amount of money represented by 40 quarters, 40 dimes, and 20 nickels is   35._____

    A. $14.50   B. $15.00   C. $15.50   D. $16.00

36. The sum of $29.61 + $101.53 + $943.64 is   36._____

    A. $983.88   B. $1074.78   C. $1174.98   D. $1341.42

37. The sum of $132.25 + $85.63 + $7056.44 is   37._____

    A. $1694.19   B. $7274.32   C. $8464.57   D. $9346.22

38. The sum of 4010 + 1271 + 23 + 838 is

    A. 6142   B. 6162   C. 6242   D. 6362

    38.____

39. What is the value of 3 twenty dollar bills, 5 ten dollar bills, 13 five dollar bills, and 43 one dollar bills?

    A. $218.00   B. $219.00   C. $220.00   D. $221.00

    39.____

40. What is the value of 8 twenty dollar bills, 13 ten dollar bills, 27 five dollar bills, 3 two dollar bills, and 43 one dollar bills?

    A. $364.00   B. $374.00   C. $474.00   D. $485.00

    40.____

41. What is the value of 6 twenty dollar bills, 8 ten dollar bills, 19 five dollar bills, and 37 one dollar bills?

    A. $232.00   B. $233.00   C. $332.00   D. $333.00

    41.____

42. What is the value of 13 twenty dollar bills, 17 ten dollar bills, 24 five dollar bills, 7 two dollar bills, and 55 one dollar bills?

    A. $594.00   B. $599.00   C. $609.00   D. $619.00

    42.____

43. What is the value of 7 half dollars, 9 quarters, 23 dimes, and 17 nickels?

    A. $7.80   B. $7.90   C. $8.80   D. $8.90

    43.____

44. What is the value of 3 one dollar coins, 3 half dollars, 7 quarters, 13 dimes, and 27 nickels?

    A. $7.80   B. $8.70   C. $8.80   D. $8.90

    44.____

45. What is the value of 73 quarters?

    A. $18.25   B. $18.50   C. $18.75   D. $19.00

    45.____

46. What is the value of 173 nickels?

    A. $8.55   B. $8.65   C. $8.75   D. $8.85

    46.____

47. In checking a book of consecutively numbered Senior Citizen tickets, you find there are no tickets between number 13,383 and 13,833.
    How many tickets are missing?

    A. 448   B. 449   C. 450   D. 451

    47.____

48. A ticket clerk begins her shift with 2,322 tickets. How many tickets will she have at the end of her shift if she sells 1,315 and collects 1,704 from the turnstiles during her shift?

    A. 2,687   B. 2,693   C. 2,711   D. 2,722

    48.____

49. A ticket clerk has three books of tickets. One contains 273 tickets, one contains 342 tickets, and one contains 159 tickets. The clerk combines the contents of the three books and then sells 217 tickets.
    How many tickets are left?

    A. 556   B. 557   C. 568   D. 991

    49.____

50. A ticket clerk has a quantity of consecutively numbered tickets. The number on the ticket   50.___
having the lowest number is 27,069. The number on the ticket having the highest number
is 27,154.
How many tickets does the clerk have?

   A. 84   B. 85   C. 86   D. 87

KEY (CORRECT ANSWERS)

1. D	11. C	21. D	31. D	41. C
2. C	12. C	22. B	32. A	42. D
3. B	13. A	23. C	33. B	43. D
4. C	14. D	24. B	34. D	44. D
5. C	15. A	25. B	35. B	45. A
6. A	16. C	26. B	36. B	46. B
7. B	17. B	27. C	37. B	47. B
8. A	18. A	28. A	38. A	48. C
9. A	19. D	29. B	39. A	49. B
10. D	20. C	30. D	40. C	50. C

SOLUTIONS TO PROBLEMS

1. 53,632 + 27,403 + 98,765 + 75,424 = 255,224

2. 76,342 + 49,050 + 21,206 + 59,989 = 206,587

3. $452.13 + $963.83 + $621.25 = $2037.21

4. 36,392 + 42,156 + 98,765 = 177,313

5. 40,125 + 87,123 + 24,689 = 151,937

6. 2379 + 4015 + 6521 + 9986 = 22901

7. 50,962 - 36,197 = 14,765

8. 90,000 - 31,928 = 58,072

9. 63,764 - 21,548 = 42,216

10. $9605.13 - $2715.96 = $6889.17

11. 76,421 - 73,101 = 3320

12. $8.25 - $6.50 = $1.75

13. (563)(.50) = 281.50

14. (.35)(1045) = 365.75

15. (25)(2513) = 62,825

16. (423)(.01) = 4.23

17. (6.70)(3.2) = 21.44

18. (630)(517) = 325,710

19. (35)(846) = 29,610

20. (823)(.05) = 41.15

21. (1690)(.10) = 169

22. 2765 / 35 = 79

23. $18.55 - $6.80 = $11.75

24. 2.75 + 4.50 + 3.60 = 10.85

25. 9.63 + 11.21 + 17.25 = 38.09

26. 112.0 + 16.9 + 3.84 = 132.74

27. 65 + (14)(13) = 247

28. $391.55 - $273.45 = $118.10

29. 2016 + 1634 - 119 = 3531

30. $367.20 + $510.00 + $402.80 = $1280.00

31. (35)(65)(15) = 34,125

32. (40)(65)(10) - 26,000

33. (43)(.50) + (26)(.25) + (71)(.10) = $35.10

34. (132)(.25) + (97)(.10) + (220)(.05) = $53.70

35. (40)(.25) + (40)(.10) + (20)(.05) = $15.00

36. $29.61 + $101.53 + $943.64 = $1074.78

37. $132.25 + $85.63 + $7056.44 = $7274.32

38. 4010 + 1271 + 23 + 838 = 6142

39. (3)($20) + (5)($10) + (13)($5) + (43)($1) + $218.00

40. (8)($20) + (13)($10) + (27)($5) + (3)($2) + (43)($1) = $474.00

41. (6)($20) + (8)($10) + (19)($5) + (37)($1) = $332.00

42. (13)($20) + (17)($10) + (24)($5) + (7)($2) + (55)($1) = $619.00

43. (7)(.50) + (9)(.25) + (23)(.10) + (17)(.05) = $8.90

44. (3)($1) + (3)(.50) + (7)(.25) + (13)(.10) + (27)(.05) = $8.90

45. (73)(.25) = $18.25

46. (173)(.05) = $8.65

47. The missing tickets are numbered 13,384 through 13,832. This represents 13,832 - 13,384 + 1 = 449 tickets.

48. 2322 - 1315 + 1704 = 2711 tickets left.

49. 273 + 342 + 159 - 217 = 557 tickets left

50. 27,154 - 27,069 + 1 = 86 tickets

NUMBER COMPARISONS

EXAMINATION SECTION

DIRECTIONS: This test consists of 200 questions in which pairs of numbers are to be examined for exactness. If the two numbers are *exactly the same*, mark the answer "A" on the line provided between the two. If they are *different*, mark the answer "B." This is a test for speed and accuracy—work as fast as you can without making mistakes.

1.	307 _____	309
2.	4605 _____	4603
3.	976 _____	979
4.	101267 _____	101267
5.	3065432 _____	30965432
6.	103345700 _____	103345700
7.	46754 _____	466754
8.	3367490 _____	3367490
9.	2779 _____	2778
10.	57394 _____	57394
11.	63801829374 _____	63801839474
12.	283577657 _____	283577657
13.	75689 _____	75689
14.	2547892026 _____	2547893026
15.	336354 _____	336254
16.	998745732 _____	998745733
17.	623 _____	623
18.	263849102983 _____	263849102983
19.	5870 _____	5870
20.	379012 _____	379012
21.	8734629 _____	8734629
22.	2549806746 _____	2549806746
23.	57802564 _____	57892564
24.	689246 _____	688246
25.	1578024683 _____	1578024683
26.	582039485618 _____	582039485618
27.	63829172630 _____	63829172639
28.	592 _____	592
29.	829374820 _____	829374820
30.	62937456 _____	63937456
31.	8293 _____	8293
32.	6382910293 _____	6382910292
33.	781928374012 _____	781928374912
34.	68293 _____	68393
35.	18203649271 _____	18293649271

36.	4820384 _____	4820384
37.	283019283745 _____	283019283745
38.	73927102 _____	73927102
39.	91029354829 _____	91029354829
40.	38291728 _____	38291728
41.	6283910293 _____	6283910203
42.	392018273648 _____	392018273848
43.	820 _____	829
44.	572937273 _____	572937373
45.	7392 _____	7392
46.	8172036 _____	8172036
47.	68391028364 _____	68391028394
48.	48293 _____	48292
49.	739201 _____	739201
50.	62839201 _____	62839211
51.	5829 _____	5820
52.	192836472829 _____	192836472829
53.	362 _____	362
54.	2039271827 _____	2039276837
55.	73829 _____	73829
56.	82739102837 _____	82739102837
57.	48891028 _____	48891028
58.	7291728 _____	7291928
59.	172839102839 _____	172839102839
60.	628192 _____	628102
61.	473829432 _____	473829432
62.	478 _____	478
63.	372816253902 _____	372816252902
64.	64829 _____	64830
65.	4739210249 _____	4739210249
66.	748362 _____	748363
67.	728354792 _____	728354772
68.	3927 _____	3927
69.	927384625 _____	927384625
70.	4628156 _____	4628158
71.	6382 _____	6392
72.	12937453829 _____	12937453829
73.	523 _____	533
74.	7263920 _____	7263920
75.	74293 _____	74293
76.	82734291 _____	82734271
77.	2739102637 _____	2739102637
78.	62810263849 _____	62810263846
79.	638291 _____	638291
80.	62831027 _____	62831027

81.	527	_____	529
82.	172438291026	_____	172438291026
83.	7253829142	_____	725382942
84.	836287	_____	836289
85.	62435162839	_____	62435162839
86.	6254	_____	6256
87.	6241526	_____	6241526
88.	1426389012	_____	1426389102
89.	825	_____	825
90.	67253917287	_____	67253917287
91.	6271	_____	6271
92.	263819253627	_____	263819253629
93.	82637	_____	82937
94.	728392736	_____	728392736
95.	62739	_____	62739
96.	728352689	_____	728352688
97.	463728	_____	463728
98.	73829176	_____	73827196
99.	4825367	_____	4825369
100.	56382018	_____	56382018
101.	789	_____	789
102.	819263728192	_____	819263728172
103.	682537289	_____	682537298
104.	7245	_____	7245
105.	82936542891	_____	82936542891
106.	4738267	_____	4738277
107.	63728	_____	63729
108.	6283628901	_____	6283628991
109.	918264	_____	918264
110.	263728192037	_____	263728192073
111.	52839102738	_____	5283910238
112.	6283	_____	6282
113.	7283529152	_____	7283529152
114.	208	_____	298
115.	82637201927	_____	8263720127
116.	15273826	_____	15273826
117.	72537	_____	73537
118.	726391027384	_____	726391027384
119.	627389	_____	627399
120.	725382910	_____	725382910
121.	46273	_____	46273
122.	629	_____	620
123.	7382517283	_____	7382517283
124.	637281	_____	639281
125.	2738261	_____	2728261

126.	627152637490 _____	627152637490
127.	73526189 _____	73526189
128.	5372 _____	5392
129.	63728142 _____	63728124
130.	4783946 _____	4783046
131.	82637281028 _____	82637281028
132.	628 _____	628
133.	7293728172 _____	7293728177
134.	7362 _____	7362
135.	927382615 _____	927382615
136.	85345 _____	85345
137.	895643278 _____	895642377
138.	726352 _____	726353
139.	7263524 _____	7263524
140.	632685 _____	632685
141.	273648293048 _____	273648293048
142.	634 _____	634
143.	7362536478 _____	7362536478
144.	7362 _____	7363
145.	7362819273 _____	7362819273
146.	63728 _____	63738
147.	63728192637 _____	63728192639
148.	728 _____	738
149.	62738291527 _____	62738291529
150.	63728192 _____	63728192
151.	73526 _____	73526
152.	7283627189 _____	7283627189
153.	627 _____	637
154.	728352617283 _____	728352617282
155.	6281 _____	6381
156.	936271826 _____	936371826
157.	82637192037 _____	82637192037
158.	527182 _____	527182
159.	6273 _____	6273
160.	726354256 _____	72635456
161.	725361552637 _____	725361555637
162.	7526378 _____	7526377
163.	685 _____	685
164.	82637481028 _____	82637481028
165.	3427 _____	3429
166.	827364933251 _____	827364933351
167.	63728 _____	63728
168.	6273846273 _____	6273846293
169.	62836 _____	6283
170.	2638496 _____	2638496

36

171.	738291627874 _____	738291627874
172.	62826454 _____	62836455
173.	42738267 _____	42738269
174.	573829 _____	573829
175.	628364728 _____	628364928
176.	725 _____	735
177.	627385 _____	627383
178.	63354 _____	63354
179.	54283902 _____	54283602
180.	7283562781 _____	7283562781
181.	62738 _____	63738
182.	727355542321 _____	72735542321
183.	263849332 _____	263849332
184.	162837 _____	163837
185.	47382912 _____	47382922
186.	628367299 _____	628367399
187.	111 _____	111
188.	11829304829 _____	11828304829
189.	4448 _____	4448
190.	333693678 _____	333693678
191.	3212 _____	3212
192.	27389223678 _____	27389223678
193.	473829 _____	473829
194.	7382937 _____	7383937
195.	3628901223 _____	3628901233
196.	5572867 _____	5572867
197.	87263543 _____	87263543
198.	3678902 _____	3678892
199.	15672839 _____	15672839
200.	9927382 _____	9927382

KEY (CORRECT ANSWERS)

1. B	41. B	81. B	121. A	161. B
2. B	42. B	82. A	122. B	162. B
3. B	43. B	83. B	123. A	163. A
4. A	44. B	84. B	124. B	164. A
5. B	45. A	85. A	125. B	165. B
6. A	46. A	86. B	126. A	166. B
7. B	47. B	87. A	127. A	167. A
8. A	48. B	88. B	128. B	168. B
9. B	49. A	89. A	129. B	169. B
10. A	50. B	90. A	130. B	170. A
11. B	51. B	91. B	131. A	171. A
12. A	52. A	92. B	132. A	172. B
13. A	53. A	93. B	133. B	173. B
14. B	54. B	94. A	134. A	174. A
15. A	55. A	95. A	135. A	175. B
16. B	56. A	96. B	136. A	176. B
17. A	57. A	97. A	137. B	177. B
18. A	58. B	98. B	138. B	178. A
19. A	59. A	99. B	139. A	179. B
20. A	60. B	100. A	140. A	180. A
21. A	61. A	101. A	141. A	181. B
22. A	62. A	102. B	142. A	182. B
23. B	63. A	103. B	143. A	183. A
24. B	64. B	104. A	144. B	184. B
25. A	65. A	105. A	145. A	185. B
26. A	66. B	106. B	146. B	186. B
27. B	67. B	107. B	147. B	187. A
28. A	68. A	108. B	148. B	188. B
29. A	69. A	109. A	149. B	189. A
30. B	70. B	110. B	150. A	190. A
31. A	71. B	111. B	151. A	191. A
32. B	72. A	112. B	152. A	192. A
33. B	73. B	113. A	153. B	193. A
34. B	74. A	114. B	154. B	194. B
35. B	75. A	115. B	155. B	195. B
36. A	76. B	116. A	156. A	196. A
37. A	77. A	117. B	157. A	197. A
38. A	78. B	118. A	158. A	198. B
39. A	79. A	119. B	159. A	199. A
40. A	80. A	120. A	160. B	200. A

NAME and NUMBER COMPARISONS

COMMENTARY

This test seeks to measure your ability and disposition to do a job carefully and accurately, your attention to exactness and preciseness of detail, your alertness and versatility in discerning similarities and differences between things, and your power in systematically handling written language symbols.

It is actually a test of your ability to do academic and/or clerical work, using the basic elements of verbal (qualitative) and mathematical (quantitative) learning - words <u>and</u> numbers.

EXAMINATION SECTION
TEST 1

DIRECTIONS: In each line across the page there are three names or numbers that are much alike. Compare the three names or numbers and decide which ones are exactly alike. *PRINT IN THE SPACE AT THE RIGHT THE LETTER:*
   A.   if all THREE names or numbers are exactly ALIKE
   B.   if only the FIRST and SECOND names or numbers are ALIKE
   C.   if only the FIRST and THIRD names or numbers are ALIKE
   D.   if only the SECOND and THIRD names or numbers are ALIKE
   E.   if ALL THREE names or numbers are DIFFERENT

1. Davis Hazen	David Hozen	David Hazen	1.____
2. Lois Appel	Lois Appel	Lois Apfel	2.____
3. June Allan	Jane Allan	Jane Allan	3.____
4. 10235	10235	10235	4.____
5. 32614	32164	32614	5.____

TEST 2

1. 2395890	2395890	2395890	1.____
2. 1926341	1926347	1926314	2.____
3. E. Owens McVey	E. Owen McVey	E. Owen McVay	3.____
4. Emily Neal Rouse	Emily Neal Rowse	Emily Neal Rowse	4.____
5. H. Merritt Audubon	H. Merriott Audubon	H. Merritt Audubon	5.____

TEST 3

1. 6219354	6219354	6219354	1.____
2. 2312793	2312793	2312793	2.____
3. 1065407	1065407	1065047	3.____
4. Francis Ransdell	Frances Ramsdell	Francis Ramsdell	4.____
5. Cornelius Detwiler	Cornelius Detwiler	Cornelius Detwiler	5.____

———

TEST 4

1. 6452054	6452654	6542054	1.____
2. 8501268	8501268	8501286	2.____
3. Ella Burk Newham	Ella Burk Newnham	Elena Burk Newnham	3.____
4. Jno. K. Ravencroft	Jno. H. Ravencroft	Jno. H. Ravencoft	4.____
5. Martin Wills Pullen	Martin Wills Pulen	Martin Wills Pullen	5.____

———

TEST 5

1. 3457988	3457986	3457986	1.____
2. 4695682	4695862	4695682	2.____
3. Stricklund Kaneydy	Sticklund Kanedy	Stricklund Kanedy	3.____
4. Joy Harlor Witner	Joy Harloe Witner	Joy Harloe Witner	4.____
5. R.M.O. Uberroth	R.M.O. Uberroth	R.N.O. Uberroth	5.____

———

TEST 6

1.	1592514	1592574	1592574	1.____
2.	2010202	2010202	2010220	2.____
3.	6177396	6177936	6177396	3.____
4.	Drusilla S. Ridgeley	Drusilla S. Ridgeley	Drusilla S. Ridgeley	4.____
5.	Andrei I. Toumantzev	Andrei I. Tourmantzev	Andrei I. Toumantzov	5.____

TEST 7

1.	5261383	5261383	5261338	1.____
2.	8125690	8126690	8125609	2.____
3.	W.E. Johnston	W.E. Johnson	W.E. Johnson	3.____
4.	Vergil L. Muller	Vergil L. Muller	Vergil L. Muller	4.____
5.	Atherton R. Warde	Asheton R. Warde	Atherton P. Warde	5.____

TEST 8

1.	013469.5	023469.5	02346.95	1.____
2.	33376	333766	333766	2.____
3.	Ling-Temco-Vought	Ling-Tenco-Vought	Ling-Temco Vought	3.____
4.	Lorilard Corp.	Lorillard Corp.	Lorrilard Corp.	4.____
5.	American Agronomics Corporation	American Agronomics Corporation	American Agronomic Corporation	5.____

TEST 9

1. 436592864	436592864	436592864	1.____
2. 197765123	197755123	197755123	2.____
3. Dewaay, Cortvriendt International S.A.	Deway, Cortvriendt International S.A.	Deway, Corturiendt International S.A.	3.____
4. Crédit Lyonnais	Crèdit Lyonnais	Crèdit Lyonais	4.____
5. Algemene Bank Nederland N.V.	Algamene Bank Nederland N.V.	Algemene Bank Naderland N.V.	5.____

———

TEST 10

1. 00032572	0.0032572	00032522	1.____
2. 399745	399745	398745	2.____
3. Banca Privata Finanziaria S.p.A.	Banca Privata Finanzaria S.P.A.	Banca Privata Finanziaria S.P.A.	3.____
4. Eastman Dillon, Union Securities & Co.	Eastman Dillon, Union Securities Co.	Eastman Dillon, Union Securities & Co.	4.____
5. Arnhold and S. Bleichroeder, Inc.	Arnhold & S. Bleichroeder, Inc.	Arnold and S. Bleichroeder, Inc.	5.____

———

TEST 11

DIRECTIONS: Answer the questions below on the basis of the following instructions: For each such numbered set of names, addresses and numbers listed in Columns I and II, select your answer from the following options:
- A: The names in Columns I and II are different
- B: The addresses in Columns I and II are different
- C: The numbers in Columns I and II are different
- D: The names, addresses and numbers are identical

	Column I	Column II	
1.	Francis Jones 62 Stately Avenue 96-12446	Francis Jones 62 Stately Avenue 96-21446	1.____
2.	Julio Montez 19 Ponderosa Road 56-73161	Julio Montez 19 Ponderosa Road 56-71361	2.____
3.	Mary Mitchell 2314 Melbourne Drive 68-92172	Mary Mitchell 2314 Melbourne Drive 68-92172	3.____
4.	Harry Patterson 25 Dunne Street 14-33430	Harry Patterson 25 Dunne Street 14-34330	4.____
5.	Patrick Murphy 171 West Hosmer Street 93-81214	Patrick Murphy 171 West Hosmer Street 93-18214	5.____

TEST 12

	Column I	Column II	
1.	August Schultz 816 St. Clair Avenue 53-40149	August Schultz 816 St. Claire Avenue 53-40149	1.____
2.	George Taft 72 Runnymede Street 47-04033	George Taft 72 Runnymede Street 47-04023	2.____
3.	Angus Henderson 1418 Madison Street 81-76375	Angus Henderson 1418 Madison Street 81-76375	3.____
4.	Carolyn Mazur 12 Riven/lew Road 38-99615	Carolyn Mazur 12 Rivervane Road 38-99615	4.____
5.	Adele Russell 1725 Lansing Lane 72-91962	Adela Russell 1725 Lansing Lane 72-91962	5.____

43

TEST 13

DIRECTIONS: The following questions are based on the instructions given below. In each of the following questions, the 3-line name and address in Column I is the master-list entry, and the 3-line entry in Column II is the information to be checked against the master list.

If there is one line that is *not* exactly alike, mark your answer A.
If there are two lines *not* exactly alike, mark your answer B.
If there are three lines *not* exactly alike, mark your answer C.
If the lines *all are* exactly alike, mark your answer D.

1. Jerome A. Jackson   Jerome A. Johnson   1.____
    1243 14th Avenue   1234 14th Avenue
    New York, N.Y. 10023   New York, N.Y. 10023

2. Sophie Strachtheim   Sophie Strachtheim   2.____
    33-28 Connecticut Ave.   33-28 Connecticut Ave.
    Far Rockaway, N.Y. 11697   Far Rockaway, N.Y. 11697

3. Elisabeth NT. Gorrell   Elizabeth NT. Gorrell   3.____
    256 Exchange St   256 Exchange St.
    New York, N.Y. 10013   New York, N.Y. 10013

4. Maria J. Gonzalez   Maria J. Gonzalez   4.____
    7516 E. Sheepshead Rd.   7516 N. Shepshead Rd.
    Brooklyn, N.Y. 11240   Brooklyn, N.Y. 11240

5. Leslie B. Brautenweiler   Leslie B. Brautenwieler   5.____
    21-57A Seller Terr.   21-75ASeilerTerr.
    Flushing, N.Y. 11367   Flushing, N.J. 11367

KEYS (CORRECT ANSWERS)

TEST 1	TEST 2	TEST 3	TEST 4	TEST 5	TEST 6	TEST 7
1. E	1. A	1. A	1. E	1. D	1. D	1. B
2. B	2. E	2. A	2. B	2. C	2. B	2. E
3. D	3. E	3. B	3. E	3. E	3. C	3. D
4. A	4. D	4. E	4. E	4. D	4. A	4. A
5. C	5. C	5. A	5. C	5. B	5. E	5. E

TEST 8	TEST 9	TEST 10	TEST 11	TEST 12	TEST 13
1. E	1. A	1. E	1. C	1. B	1. B
2. D	2. D	2. B	2. C	2. C	2. D
3. E	3. E	3. E	3. D	3. D	3. B
4. E	4. E	4. C	4. C	4. B	4. A
5. B	5. E	5. E	5. C	5. A	5. C

NAME AND NUMBER CHECKING

EXAMINATION SECTION
TEST 1

DIRECTIONS: This test is designed to measure your speed and accuracy. You are urged to work both quickly and accurately and to do correctly as many lists as you can in the time allowed. The test consists of lists of pairs of names and numbers. Count the number of IDENTICAL pairs in each list. Then, select the correct number, 1, 2, 3, 4, or 5, and indicate your choice by circling the corresponding number on your answer paper, Two sample questions are presented for your guidance, together with the correct solutions.

SAMPLE QUESTIONS

CIRCLE
CORRECT ANSWER

SAMPLE LIST A

Adelphi College	- Adelphia College	1 2 3 4 5
Braxton Corp.	- Braxeton Corp.	
Wassaic State School	- Wassaic State School	
Central Islip State Hospital	- Central Isllip State	
Greenwich House	- Greenwich House	

NOTE that there are only two correct pairs - Wassaic State School and Greenwich House. Therefore, the CORRECT answer is 2.

SAMPLE LIST B

78453694	- 78453684	1 2 3 4 5
784530	- 784530	
533	- 534	
67845	- 67845	
2368745	- 2368755	

NOTE that there are only two correct pairs - 784530 and 67845. Therefore, the COR-RECT answer is 2.

LIST 1

98654327	- 98654327	1 2 3 4 5
74932564	- 74922564	
61438652	- 61438652	
01297653	- 01287653	
1865439765	- 1865439765	

LIST 2

478362	- 478363	1 2 3 4 5
278354792	- 278354772	
9327	- 9327	
297384625	- 27384625	
6428156	- 6428158	

CIRCLE
CORRECT ANSWER

LIST 3

Abbey House	- Abbey House	1 2 3 4 5
Actors' Fund Home	- Actor's Fund Home	
Adrian Memorial	- Adrian Memorial	
A. Clayton Powell Home	- Clayton Powell House	
Abott E. Kittredge Club	- Abbott E. Kitteredge Club	

LIST 4

3682	- 3692	1 2 3 4 5
21937453829	- 31937453829	
723	- 733	
2763920	- 2763920	
47293	- 47293	

LIST 5

Adra House	- Adra House	1 2 3 4 5
Adolescents' Court	- Adolescents' Court	
Cliff Villa	- Cliff Villa	
Clark Neighborhood House	- Clark Neighborhood House	
Alma Mathews House	- Alma Mathews House	

LIST 6

28734291	- 28734271	1 2 3 4 5
63810263849	- 63810263846	
26831027	- 26831027	
368291	- 368291	
7238102637	- 7238102637	

LIST 7

Albion State T.S.	- Albion State T.C.	1 2 3 4 5
Clara de Hirsch Home	- Clara De Hirsch Home	
Alice Carrington Royce	- Alice Carington Royce	
Alice Chopin Nursery	- Alice Chapin Nursery	
Lighthouse Eye Clinic	- Lighthouse Eye Clinic	

LIST 8

327	- 329	1 2 3 4 5
712438291026	- 712438291026	
2753829142	- 275382942	
826287	- 826289	
26435162839	- 26435162839	

LIST 9

Letchworth Village	- Letchworth Village	1 2 3 4 5
A.A.A.E. Inc.	- A.A.A.E. Inc.	
Clear Pool Camp	- Clear Pool Camp	
A.M.M.L.A. Inc.	- A.M.M.L.A. Inc.	
J.G. Harbard	- J.G. Harbord	

LIST 10

8254	- 8256	1 2 3 4 5
2641526	- 2641526	
4126389012	- 4126389102	
725	- 725	
76253917287	- 76253917287	

LIST 11

Attica State Prison	- Attica State Prison	1 2 3 4 5
Nellie Murrah	- Nellie Murrah	
Club Marshall	- Club Marshal	
Assissium Casea-Maria	- Assissium Casa-Maria	
The Homestead	- The Homestead	

LIST 12

2691	- 2691	1 2 3 4 5
623819253627	- 623819253629	
28637	- 28937	
278392736	- 278392736	
52739	- 52739	

LIST 13

A.I.C.P. Boys Camp	- A.I.C.P. Boy's Camp	1 2 3 4 5
Einar Chrystie	- Einar Christyie	
Astoria Center	- Astoria Center	
G. Frederick Brown	- G. Federick Browne	
Vacation Service	- Vacation Services	

LIST 14

728352689	- 728352688	1 2 3 4 5
643728	- 643728	
37829176	- 37827196	
8425367	- 8425369	
65382018	- 65382018	

LIST 15

E.S. Streim	- E.S. Strim	1 2 3 4 5
Charles E. Higgins	- Charles E. Higgins	
Baluvelt, N.Y.	- Blauwelt, N.Y.	
Roberta Magdalen	- Roberto Magdalen	
Ballard School	- Ballard School	

LIST 16

7382	- 7392	1 2 3 4 5
281374538299	- 291374538299	
623	- 633	
6273730	- 6273730	
63392	- 63392	

LIST 17

		1	2	3	4	5
Orrin Otis	- Orrin Otis					
Barat Settlement	- Barat Settlemen					
Emmanuel House	- Emmanuel House					
William T. McCreery	- William T. McCreery					
Seamen's Home	- Seaman's Home					

LIST 18

		1	2	3	4	5
72824391	- 72834371					
3729106237	- 37291106237					
82620163849	- 82620163846					
37638921	- 37638921					
82631027	- 82631027					

LIST 19

		1	2	3	4	5
Commonwealth Fund	- Commonwealth Fund					
Anne Johnsen	- Anne Johnson					
Bide-a-Wee Home	- Bide-a-Wee Home					
Riverdale-on-Hudson	- Riverdal-on-Hudson					
Bialystoker Home	- Bailystoker Home					

LIST 20

		1	2	3	4	5
9271	- 9271					
392918352627	- 392018852629					
72637	- 72637					
927392736	- 927392736					
92739	- 92739					

LIST 21

		1	2	3	4	5
Charles M. Stump	- Charles M. Stump					
Bourne Workshop	- Buorne Workshop					
B'nai Bi'rith	- B'nai Brith					
Poppenhuesen Institute	- Poppenheusen Institute					
Consular Service	- Consular Service					

LIST 22

		1	2	3	4	5
927352689	- 927352688					
647382	- 648382					
93729176	- 93727196					
649536718	- 649536718					
5835367	- 5835369					

LIST 23

		1	2	3	4	5
L.S. Bestend	- L.S. Bestent					
Hirsch Mfg. Co.	- Hircsh Mfg. Co.					
F.H. Storrs	- F.P. Storrs					
Camp Wassaic	- Camp Wassaic					
George Ballingham	- George Ballingham					

LIST 24

372846392048	- 372846392048
334	- 334
7283524678	- 7283524678
7283	- 7283
7283629372	- 7283629372

1 2 3 4 5

LIST 25

Dr. Stiles Company	- Dr. Stills Company
Frances Hunsdon	- Frances Hunsdon
Northrop Barrert	- Nothrup Barrent
J. D. Brunjes	- J. D. Brunjes
Theo. Claudel & Co.	- Theo. Claudel co.

1 2 3 4 5

———

KEY (CORRECT ANSWERS)

1.	3	11.	3
2.	1	12.	3
3.	2	13.	1
4.	2	14.	2
5.	5	15.	2
6.	3	16.	2
7.	1	17.	3
8.	2	18.	2
9.	4	19.	2
10.	3	20.	4

21.	2
22.	1
23.	2
24.	5
25.	2

———

TEST 2

DIRECTIONS: This test is designed to measure your speed and accuracy. You are urged to work both quickly and accurately and to do correctly as many lists as you can in the time allowed. The test consists of lists of pairs of names and numbers. Count the number of IDENTICAL pairs in each list. Then, select the correct number, 1, 2, 3, 4, or 5, and indicate your choice by circling the corresponding number on your answer paper, Two sample questions are presented for your guidance, together with the correct solutions.

LIST 1

82728	- 82738	CIRCLE
82736292637	- 82736292639	CORRECT ANSWER
728	- 738	1 2 3 4 5
83926192527	- 83726192529	
82736272	- 82736272	

LIST 2

L. Pietri	- L. Pietri	
Mathewson, L.F.	- Mathewson, L.F.	
Funk & Wagnall	- Funk &. Wagnalls	1 2 3 4 5
Shimizu, Sojio	- Shimizu, Sojio	
Filing Equipment Bureau	- Filing Equipment Buraeu	

LIST 3

63801829374	- 63801839474	
283577657	- 283577657	
65689	- 65689	1 2 3 4 5
3457892026	- 3547893026	
2779	- 2778	

LIST 4

August Caille	- August Caille	
The Well-Fare Service	- The Wel-Fare Service	
K.L.M. Process Co.	- R.L.M. Process Co.	1 2 3 4 5
Merrill Littell	- Merrill Littell	
Dodd & Sons	- Dodd & Son	

LIST 5

998745732	- 998745733	
723	- 723	
463849102983	- 463849102983	1 2 3 4 5
8570	- 8570	
279012	- 279012	

LIST 6

M. A. Wender	- M.A. Winder	
Minneapolis Supply Co.	- Minneapolis Supply Co.	
Beverly Hills Corp	- Beverley Hills Corp.	1 2 3 4 5
Trafalgar Square	- Trafalgar Square	
Phifer, D.T.	- Phiefer, D.T.	

LIST 7

7834629	- 7834629	1 2 3 4 5
3549806746	- 3549806746	
97802564	- 97892564	
689246	- 688246	
2578024683	- 2578024683	

LIST 8

Scadrons'	- Scadrons'	1 2 3 4 5
Gensen & Bro.	- Genson & Bro.	
Firestone Co.	- Firestone Co.	
H.L. Eklund ·	- H.L. Eklund	
Oleomargarine Co.	- Oleomargarine Co.	

LIST 9

782039485618	- 782039485618	1 2 3 4 5
53829172639	- 63829172639	
892	- 892	
82937482	- 829374820	
52937456	- 53937456	

LIST 10

First Nat'l Bank	- First Nat'l Bank	1 2 3 4 5
Sedgwick Machine Works	- Sedgewick Machine Works	
Hectographia Co.	- Hectographia Corp.	
Levet Bros.	- Levet Bros.	
Multistamp Co.,Inc.	- Multistamp Co.,Inc.	

LIST 11

7293	- 7293	1 2 3 4 5
6382910293	- 6382910292	
981928374012	- 981928374912	
58293	- 58393	
18203649271	- 283019283745	

LIST 12

Lowrey Lb'r Co.	- Lowrey Lb'r Co.	1 2 3 4 5
Fidelity Service	- Fidelity Service	
Reumann, J.A.	- Reumann, J.A.	
Duophoto Ltd.	- Duophotos Ltd.	
John Jarratt	- John Jaratt	

LIST 13

6820384	- 6820384	1 2 3 4 5
383019283745	- 383019283745	
63927102	- 63928102	
91029354829	- 91029354829	
58291728	- 58291728	

LIST 14

Standard Press Co.	- Standard Press Co.	1 2 3 4 5
Reliant Mf'g. Co.	- Relant Mf'g Co.	
M.C. Lynn	- M.C. Lynn	
J. Fredericks Company	- G. Fredericks Company	
Wandermann, B.S.	- Wanderman, B.S.	

LIST 15

4283910293	- 4283010203	1 2 3 4 5
992018273648	- 992018273848	
620	- 629	
752937273	- 752937373	
5392	- 5392	

LIST 16

Waldorf Hotel	- Waldorf Hotel	1 2 3 4 5
Aaron Machinery Co.	- Aaron Machinery Co.	
Caroline Ann Locke	- Caroline Anne Locke	
McCabe Mfg. Co.	- McCabe Mfg. Co.	
R.L. Landres	- R.L. Landers	

LIST 17

68391028364	- 68391028394	1 2 3 4 5
68293	- 68293	
739201	- 739201	
72839201	- 72839211	
739917	- 739719	

LIST 18

Balsam M.M.	- Balsamm, M.M.	1 2 3 4 5
Steinway & Co.	- Stienway & M. Co.	
Eugene Elliott	- Eugene A. Elliott	
Leonard Loan Co.	- Leonard Loan Co.	
Frederick Morgan	- Frederick Morgen	

LIST 19

8929	- 9820	1 2 3 4 5
392836472829	- 392836472829	
462	- 462 2039271	
827	- 2039276837	
53829	- 54829	

LIST 20

Danielson's Hofbrau	- Danielson's Hafbrau	1 2 3 4 5
Edward A. Truarme	- Edward A. Truame	
Insulite Co.	- Insulite Co.	
Reisler Shoe Corp,	- Rielser Shoe Corp.	
L.L. Thompson	- L.L. Thompson	

CIRCLE
CORRECT ANSWER

LIST 21

92839102837	- 92839102837	1 2 3 4 5
58891028	- 58891028	
7291728	- 7291928	
272839102839	- 272839102839	
428192	- 428102	

LIST 22

K.L. Veiller	- K.L. Veiller	1 2 3 4 5
Webster, Roy	- Webster, Ray	
Drasner Spring Co.	- Drasner Spring Co.	
Edward J. Cravenport	- Edward J. Cravanport	
Harold Field	- Harold A. Field	

LIST 23

2293	- 2293	1 2 3 4 5
4283910293	- 5382910292	
871928374012	- 871928374912	
68293	- 68393	
8120364927	- 81293649271	

LIST 24

Tappe, Inc	- Tappe, Inc.	1 2 3 4 5
A.M. Wentingworth	- A.M. Wentinworth	
Scott A. Elliott	- Scott A. Elliott	
Echeverria Corp.	- Echeverria Corp.	
Bradford Victor Company	- Bradford Victer Company	

LIST 25

4820384	- 4820384	1 2 3 4 5
393019283745	- 283919283745	
63927102	- 63927102	
91029354829	- 91029354829	
48291728	- 48291728	

KEY (CORRECT ANSWERS)

1.	1		11.	1
2.	3		12.	3
3.	2		13.	4
4.	2		14.	2
5.	4		15.	1
6.	2		16.	3
7.	3		17.	2
8.	4		18.	1
9.	2		19.	1
10.	3		20.	2

21.	3
22.	2
23.	1
24.	2
25.	4

INTERPRETING STATISTICAL DATA
GRAPHS, CHARTS AND TABLES

EXAMINATION SECTION
TEST 1

DIRECTIONS: Each question or incomplete statement is followed by several suggested answers or completions. Select the one that BEST answers the question or completes the statement. *PRINT THE LETTER OF THE CORRECT ANSWER IN THE SPACE AT THE RIGHT.*

Questions 1-3.

DIRECTIONS: Questions 1 through 3 are to be answered SOLELY on the basis of the information contained in the following chart.

	New York	Bridge-port	Dan-bury	Hart-ford	New Haven	New London	Stam-ford	Water-bury
	CHART A							
	MILEAGE BETWEEN NEW YORK AND POINTS IN NEARBY CONNECTICUT							
New York	--	61	66	115	80	132	39	91
Bridgeport	61	--	27	54	19	71	22	30
Danbury	66	27	--	57	33	85	31	30
Hartford	115	54	57	--	37	44	76	27
New Haven	80	19	33	37	--	52	41	21
New London	132	71	85	44	52	--	93	62
Stamford	39	22	31	76	41	93	--	52
Waterbury	91	30	30	27	21	62	52	--

1. According to Chart A, the TOTAL mileage on a continuous trip from New York to Danbury, to Waterbury, to New London, to New York would be _____ miles.   1._____

   A. 280   B. 290   C. 316   D. 294

2. According to Chart A, the mileage between New Haven and New London is the same as the mileage between _____ and _____.   2._____

   A. Danbury; Hartford   B. Hartford; New London
   C. Stamford; New Haven   D. Waterbury; Stamford

3. According to Chart A, which of the following pairs of cities are CLOSEST to each other?   3._____

   A. Bridgeport and Hartford   B. New York and Bridgeport
   C. Hartford and Danbury   D. New Haven and New London

KEY (CORRECT ANSWERS)

1. B
2. D
3. D

TEST 2

Questions 1-4.

DIRECTIONS: Questions 1 through 4 are to be answered SOLELY on the basis of the information given in the traffic volume table below.

TRAFFIC VOLUME COUNTS				
	Main Street		Cross Street	
Time (A.M.)	Northbound	Southbound	Eastbound	Westbound
7:00 - 7:15	100	100	70	60
7:15 - 7:30	110	100	80	70
7:30 - 7:45	150	140	110	100
7:45 - 8:00	170	160	140	130
8:00 - 8:15	210	190	120	110
8:15 - 8:30	180	170	90	80
8:30 - 8:45	160	140	70	60
8:45 - 9:00	150	160	70	50
9:00 - 9:15	140	150	50	50
9:15 - 9:30	130	120	40	20
9:30 - 9:45	120	110	30	30
9:45 - 10:00	120	100	30	30

1. The hour during which traffic, moving in both directions on Main Street, reached its PEAK was   1.____

     A. 7:30 - 8:30   B. 7:45 - 8:45
     C. 8:00 - 9:00   D. 8:15 - 9:15

2. The hour during which traffic volume, moving in both directions on Cross Street, reached its PEAK was   2.____

     A. 7:30 - 8:30   B. 7:45 - 8:45
     C. 8:00 - 9:00   D. 8:15 - 9:15

3. The HIGHEST average hourly volume over the three-hour period 7:00 to 10:00 was recorded for   3.____

     A. Main Street northbound   B. Main Street southbound
     C. Cross Street eastbound   D. Cross Street westbound

4. The PEAK 15-minute traffic volume for all directions of travel occurred between   4.____

     A. 7:30 - 7:45   B. 7:45 - 8:00
     C. 8:00 - 8:15   D. 8:15 - 8:30

KEY (CORRECT ANSWERS)

1. B
2. A
3. A
4. C

———

TEST 3

Questions 1-4.

DIRECTIONS: Questions 1 through 4 are to be answered SOLELY on the basis of the sketch below.

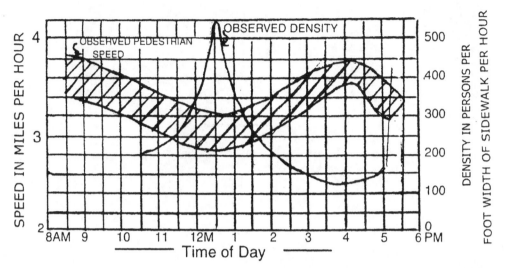

1. Assuming a 10' wide sidewalk, the number of people that would pass the given point at 12:00 Noon in 10 minutes is MOST NEARLY   1._____

    A. 580   B. 680   C. 780   D. 880

2. At 10:00 A.M., you could expect a person to be walking at a speed   2._____

    A. of 3 miles per hour
    B. between 300 and 420 feet per hour
    C. between 3.2 and 3.65 miles per hour
    D. of 4.5 feet per second

3. The highest average number of people using the sidewalk will USUALLY occur at   3._____

    A. 9 A.M.   B. 12:30 P.M.   C. 4 P.M.   D. 5 P.M.

4. Of the following statements relating to the diagram, the one that is MOST NEARLY COR-   4._____
    RECT is

    A. the minimum walking speed observed is 2 miles per hour
    B. data for the survey was taken continuously for 24 hours
    C. as the number of people using the sidewalk increases, the speed at which they walk decreases
    D. the minimum observed density is 300 people per hour per foot width of sidewalk

_____

KEY (CORRECT ANSWERS)

1. A
2. C
3. B
4. C

———

TEST 4

Questions 1-6.

DIRECTIONS: Questions 1 through 6 are to be answered SOLELY on the basis of the information given in Figure I below.

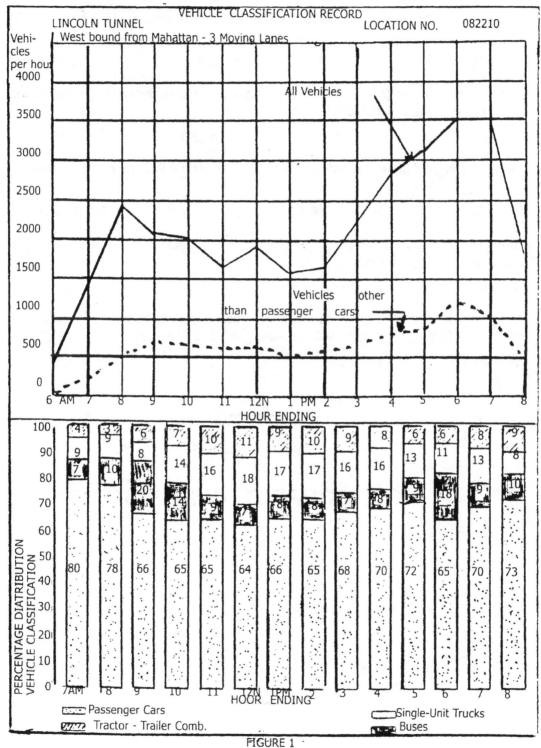

FIGURE 1

1. The total number of all vehicles traveling through the Lincoln Tunnel westbound from Manhattan between the hours of 6 A.M. and 12 Noon is MOST NEARLY

   A. 5,500   B. 7,500   C. 9,500   D. 11,500

1.____

2. The number of passenger cars recorded during the hour ending at 7 P.M. was MOST NEARLY

   A. 235   B. 1,160   C. 2,450   D. 3,500

2.____

3. Excluding passenger cars, the average number of vehicles per moving lane recorded during the peak hour was MOST NEARLY

   A. 420   B. 1,180   C. 1,250   D. 3,550

3.____

4. The percentage of buses recorded between 6 A.M. and 8 P.M. ranged between _____ and _____.

   A. 3%; 11%   B. 8%; 18%   C. 6%; 20%   D. 64%; 80%

4.____

5. During the study period, the percentage of single unit trucks EXCEEDED the percentage of buses for _____ hours.

   A. 4   B. 5   C. 9   D. 10

5.____

6. For all vehicles reported, the recorded traffic volume during the morning peak hour was MOST NEARLY _____ of the volume during the evening peak hour.

   A. 40%   B. 50%   C. 60%   D. 70%

6.____

KEY (CORRECT ANSWERS)

1. D
2. C
3. A
4. C
5. C
6. D

INTERPRETING STATISTICAL DATA
GRAPHS, CHARTS AND TABLES
EXAMINATION SECTION
TEST 1

DIRECTIONS: Each question or incomplete statement is followed by several suggested answers or completions. Select the one that BEST answers the question or completes the statement. *PRINT THE LETTER OF THE CORRECT ANSWER IN THE SPACE AT THE RIGHT.*

Questions 1-8.

DIRECTIONS: Questions 1 through 8 are to be answered SOLELY on the basis of the REPORT OF HOURLY TURNSTILE READINGS below. The changes in the readings for each turnstile from hour to hour give the number of passengers who passed through that turnstile for each hour.

REPORT OF HOURLY TURNSTILE READINGS

TURN-STILE NO.	READ AT 1 AM	READ AT 2 AM	READ AT 3 AM	READ AT 4 AM	READ AT 5 AM	READ AT 6 AM	READ AT 7 AM	READ AT 8 AM	DIFFER-ENCE FOR ENTIRE PERIOD
1	12319	12320	12326	12359	12367	12612	12913	13128	809
2	9121	9131	9217	9389	10146	10352	10465	10529	1408
3	13475	13484	13604	13718	13869		14207	14496	1021
4	14097	14099	14104	14112	14143	14287	14397	14601	
TOTAL	49012	49034	49251	49578		51170	51982	52754	3742

1. How many passengers entered through Turnstile No. 2 between 3 AM and 7 AM?   1.____

   A. 1,247   B. 1,248   C. 1,257   D. 1,258

2. What was the TOTAL of the readings of the four turnstiles at 5 AM?   2.____

   A. 50,404   B. 50,506   C. 50,525   D. 50,637

3. How many passengers entered through Turnstile No. 1 and No. 3 between 2 AM and 4 AM?   3.____

   A. 273   B. 282   C. 291   D. 297

4. What was the reading of Turnstile No. 3 at 6 AM?   4.____

   A. 13,875   B. 13,887   C. 13,902   D. 13,919

5. What was the difference in readings for the entire period for Turnstile No. 4?   5.____

   A. 504   B. 513   C. 605   D. 614

6. How many passengers entered through the four turnstiles between 6 AM and 8 AM?   6.____

    A. 1,574   B. 1,584   C. 1,674   D. 1,684

7. How many passengers entered through Turnstile No. 1 between 1 AM and 7 AM?   7.____

    A. 594   B. 597   C. 603   D. 604

8. How many passengers entered through Turnstile No. 2 and No. 4 between 5 AM and 8 AM?   8.____

    A. 796   B. 822   C. 841   D. 851

KEY (CORRECT ANSWERS)

1.	B	5.	A
2.	C	6.	B
3.	A	7.	A
4.	D	8.	C

TEST 2

Questions 1-5.

DIRECTIONS: Questions 1 through 5 are to be answered on the basis of the following chart.

HOURLY TURNSTILE READINGS

TURNSTILE NO.	7:00 AM	8:00 AM	9:00 AM	10:00 AM	11:00 AM
1	37111	37905	38342	38451	38485
2	78432	79013	79152	79237	79306
3	45555	45921	45989	46143	46233
4	89954	90063	90121	90242	90299

1. The TOTAL number of passengers using Turnstile No. 1 from 7:00 AM to 11:00 AM is   1.____

   A. 580   B. 794   C. 1374   D. 1594

2. The turnstile which registered the LARGEST number of fares from 7:00 AM to 8:00 AM is   2.____
   No.

   A. 1   B. 2   C. 3   D. 4

3. The TOTAL number of passengers using all four turnstiles between 10:00 AM and 11:00   3.____
   AM is

   A. 57   B. 250   C. 396   D. 3271

4. Turnstile No. 4 registered the HIGHEST number of passengers between _____ AM and   4.____
   _____ AM.

   A. 7:00; 8:00   B. 8:00; 9:00
   C. 9:00; 10:00   D. 10:00; 11:00

5. The turnstile which registered the LOWEST number of passengers between 8:00 AM   5.____
   and 9:00 AM is No.

   A. 1   B. 2   C. 3   D. 4

KEY (CORRECT ANSWERS)

1. C
2. A
3. B
4. C
5. D

TEST 3

Questions 1-3.

DIRECTIONS: Questions 1 through 3 are to be answered on the basis of the information contained in the FARE REPORT below. A Railroad Clerk records the reading of the counter of each turnstile when he comes on duty, and does the same again one hour before he goes off duty. (The readings of the counters he records when he comes on duty are obtained from the Railroad Clerk who is going off duty.)

FARE REPORT

Beginning At <u>0700</u>	Hours _____ Mo. _____ Day _____ 19 _____
Tour Ending At <u>1500</u>	Hours _____ Mo. _____ Day _____ 19 _____
Division _____	Station _____

Turnstile	Opening Reading at <u>0600</u>		Closing Reading at <u>1400</u>		Difference	
1	06	343	07	214		871
2			54	472	1	615
3	91	703	92	365		
4	17	925	20	107	2	182
5						
6						
7						
8						
9						
10						
TOTAL	168	828			5	330
ADD	Hand collections/Unregistered fares (explain in remarks)					
	TOTAL FARES					

1. What was the opening reading of Turnstile No. 2?

    A. 52,766   B. 52,857   C. 52,868   D. 53,857

2. What was the difference between the opening reading and the closing reading of Turnstile No. 3?

    A. 562   B. 568   C. 662   D. 668

1.____

2.____

3. What was the TOTAL of the closing readings of all four turnstiles?   3.____

    A. 163,498   B. 173,158   C. 173,498   D. 174,158

KEY (CORRECT ANSWERS)

    1. B
    2. C
    3. D

INTERPRETING STATISTICAL DATA
GRAPHS, CHARTS AND TABLES
EXAMINATION SECTION
TEST 1

DIRECTIONS: Each question or incomplete statement is followed by several suggested answers or completions. Select the one that BEST answers the question or completes the statement. *PRINT THE LETTER OF THE CORRECT ANSWER IN THE SPACE AT THE RIGHT.*

Questions 1-8.

DIRECTIONS: Questions 1 through 8 are to be answered SOLELY on the basis of the REPORT OF HOURLY TURNSTILE READINGS below. The changes in the readings for each turnstile from hour to hour give the number of passengers who passed through that turnstile for each hour.

REPORT OF HOURLY TURNSTILE READINGS

TURN-STILE NO.	READ AT 1 AM	READ AT 2 AM	READ AT 3 AM	READ AT 4 AM	READ AT 5 AM	READ AT 6 AM	READ AT 7 AM	READ AT 8 AM	DIFFER-ENCE FOR ENTIRE PERIOD
1	12319	12320	12326	12359	12367	12612	12913	13128	809
2	9121	9131	9217	9389	10146	10352	10465	10529	1408
3	13475	13484	13604	13718	13869		14207	14496	1021
4	14097	14099	14104	14112	14143	14287	14397	14601	
TOTAL	49012	49034	49251	49578		51170	51982	52754	3742

1. How many passengers entered through Turnstile No. 2 between 3 AM and 7 AM?   1.____

    A. 1,247   B. 1,248   C. 1,257   D. 1,258

2. What was the TOTAL of the readings of the four turnstiles at 5 AM?   2.____

    A. 50,404   B. 50,506   C. 50,525   D. 50,637

3. How many passengers entered through Turnstile No. 1 and No. 3 between 2 AM and 4 AM?   3.____

    A. 273   B. 282   C. 291   D. 297

4. What was the reading of Turnstile No. 3 at 6 AM?   4.____

    A. 13,875   B. 13,887   C. 13,902   D. 13,919

5. What was the difference in readings for the entire period for Turnstile No. 4?   5.____

    A. 504   B. 513   C. 605   D. 614

6. How many passengers entered through the four turnstiles between 6 AM and 8 AM?   6.____

    A. 1,574   B. 1,584   C. 1,674   D. 1,684

7. How many passengers entered through Turnstile No. 1 between 1 AM and 7 AM?   7.____

    A. 594   B. 597   C. 603   D. 604

8. How many passengers entered through Turnstile No. 2 and No. 4 between 5 AM and 8 AM?   8.____

    A. 796   B. 822   C. 841   D. 851

KEY (CORRECT ANSWERS)

1.	B		5.	A
2.	C		6.	B
3.	A		7.	A
4.	D		8.	C

TEST 2

Questions 1-5.

DIRECTIONS: Questions 1 through 5 are to be answered on the basis of the following chart.

HOURLY TURNSTILE READINGS

TURNSTILE NO.	7:00 AM	8:00 AM	9:00 AM	10:00 AM	11:00 AM
1	37111	37905	38342	38451	38485
2	78432	79013	79152	79237	79306
3	45555	45921	45989	46143	46233
4	89954	90063	90121	90242	90299

1. The TOTAL number of passengers using Turnstile No. 1 from 7:00 AM to 11:00 AM is   1.____

   A. 580   B. 794   C. 1374   D. 1594

2. The turnstile which registered the LARGEST number of fares from 7:00 AM to 8:00 AM is   2.____
   No.

   A. 1   B. 2   C. 3   D. 4

3. The TOTAL number of passengers using all four turnstiles between 10:00 AM and 11:00   3.____
   AM is

   A. 57   B. 250   C. 396   D. 3271

4. Turnstile No. 4 registered the HIGHEST number of passengers between _____ AM and   4.____
   _____ AM.

   A. 7:00; 8:00   B. 8:00; 9:00
   C. 9:00; 10:00   D. 10:00; 11:00

5. The turnstile which registered the LOWEST number of passengers between 8:00 AM   5.____
   and 9:00 AM is No.

   A. 1   B. 2   C. 3   D. 4

KEY (CORRECT ANSWERS)

1. C
2. A
3. B
4. C
5. D

TEST 3

Questions 1-3.

DIRECTIONS: Questions 1 through 3 are to be answered on the basis of the information contained in the FARE REPORT below. A Railroad Clerk records the reading of the counter of each turnstile when he comes on duty, and does the same again one hour before he goes off duty. (The readings of the counters he records when he comes on duty are obtained from the Railroad Clerk who is going off duty.)

FARE REPORT

| Beginning At 0700 | Hours _____ Mo. _____ Day _____ 19 _____ |
| Tour Ending At 1500 | Hours _____ Mo. _____ Day _____ 19 _____ |
| Division _____ Station _____ |

Turnstile	Opening Reading at 0600		Closing Reading at 1400		Difference	
1	06	343	07	214		871
2			54	472	1	615
3	91	703	92	365		
4	17	925	20	107	2	182
5						
6						
7						
8						
9						
10						
TOTAL	168	828			5	330
ADD	Hand collections/Unregistered fares (explain in remarks)					
	TOTAL FARES					

1. What was the opening reading of Turnstile No. 2?   1.____

   A. 52,766   B. 52,857   C. 52,868   D. 53,857

2. What was the difference between the opening reading and the closing reading of Turnstile No. 3?   2.____

   A. 562   B. 568   C. 662   D. 668

3. What was the TOTAL of the closing readings of all four turnstiles?   3.____

    A. 163,498   B. 173,158   C. 173,498   D. 174,158

KEY (CORRECT ANSWERS)

    1. B
    2. C
    3. D

EXAMINATION SECTION
TEST 1

DIRECTIONS: Each question or incomplete statement is followed by several suggested answers or completions. Select the one that BEST answers the question or completes the statement. *PRINT THE LETTER OF THE CORRECT ANSWER IN THE SPACE AT THE RIGHT.*

Questions 1 -7.

DIRECTIONS: Questions 1 through 7 inclusive refer to the Tabulation of Turnstile Readings shown below, and to the note given beneath the tabulation. Refer to this tabulation and the note in answering these questions.

TABULATION OF TURNSTILE READINGS

Turnstile Number	TURNSTILE READINGS AT					
	5:30 A.M.	6:00 A.M.	7:00 A.M.	8:00 A.M.	9:00 A.M.	9:30 A.M.
1	79078	79090	79225	79590	79860	79914
2	24915	24930	25010	25441	25996	26055
3	39509	39530	39736	40533	41448	41515
4	58270	58291	58396	58958	59729	59807
5	43371	43378	43516	43888	44151	44217

NOTE: 1. The turnstiles register the number of passengers.

1. The number of passengers using turnstile No. 1 from 8:00 A.M. to 9:00 A.M. was   1.____

   A.   150   B.   270   C.   350   D.   370

2. The total number of passengers using turnstile No. 5 from opening to closing was   2.____

   A.   846   B.   1140   C.   1537   D.   2005

3. The number of passengers using turnstile No. 2 in the last half hour was   3.____

   A.   59   B.   67   C.   270   D.   314

4. The *MOST* used turnstile from opening to closing was No.   4.____

   A.   2   B.   3   C.   4   D.   5

5. The turnstile used by the *LEAST* passengers from 6:00 A.M. to 7:00 A.M. was No.   5.____

   A.   4   B.   3   C.   2   D.   1

6. From 5:30 A.M. to 7:00 A.M. the railroad clerk sold exactly 525 tokens. The cash taken in for the 525 tokens was   6.____

   A. $787.50   B. $525.00   C. $157.50   D. $57.50

7. The peak load on turnstile No. 5 is between   7._____

     A.   5:30 A.M. and 6:00 A.M.   B.   6:00 A.M. and 7:00 A.M.
     C.   7:00 A.M. and 8:00 A.M.   D.   8:00 A.M. and 9:00 A.M.

KEY (CORRECT ANSWERS)

1. B
2. A
3. A
4. B
5. C
6. B
7. C

TEST 2

DIRECTIONS: Each question or incomplete statement is followed by several suggested answers or completions. Select the one that BEST answers the question or completes the statement. *PRINT THE LETTER OF THE CORRECT ANSWER IN THE SPACE AT THE RIGHT.*

Questions 1 -7.

DIRECTIONS: Questions 1 through 7 inclusive refer to the Tabulation of Turnstile Readings shown below, and to the note given beneath the tabulation. Refer to this tabulation and the note in answering these questions

TABULATION OF TURNSTILE READINGS

Turnstile Number	TURNSTILE READINGS AT					
	5:30 A.M.	6:00 A.M.	7:00 A.M.	8:00 A.M.	9:00 A.M.	10:00 A.M.
1	38921	38931	39064	39435	39704	39843
2	67463	67486	67592	68148	68917	69058
3	65387	65408	65611	66414	67324	67461
4	22538	22542	22631	23061	23613	23720

NOTE: 1. Turnstiles are operated by tokens costing $1.00 each.
2. The subway entrance at which these turnstiles are located is open, with a railroad clerk on duty, from 5:30 A.M. to 10:00 A.M.

1. The number of passengers using turnstile No. 3 from 7:00 A.M. to 8:00 A.M. was   1.____

   A.   203   B.   803   C.   910   D.   1197

2. The turnstile used by the *MOST* passengers from 8:00 A.M. to 9:00 A.M. was No.   2.____

   A.   1   B.   2   C.   3   D.   4

3. The number of passengers using turnstile No. 4 in the *FIRST* half hour was   3.____

   A.   4   B.   10   C.   21   D.   23

4. The total number of passengers using turnstile No. 2 from opening to closing was   4.____

   A.   922   B.   1182   C.   1595   D.   2074

5. The *MOST* used turnstile from opening to closing was No.   5.____

   A.   1   B.   2   C.   3   D.   4

6. From 8:00 A.M. to 9:00 A.M. the railroad clerk sold exactly 1000 tokens, while the turnstile readings, for the four turnstiles, show that a total of 2500 passengers passed through them in the same period. The number of passengers who purchased tokens was MOST probably   6.____

   A.   less than 1000   B.   exactly 1000
   C.   between 1000 and 1500   D.   exactly 2500

7.   The cash taken in for the 1000 tokens of Question 6 was   7.____

    A. $15.00   B. $100.00   C. $1000.00   D. $1500.00

KEY (CORRECT ANSWERS)

1.   B
2.   C
3.   A
4.   C
5.   C
6.   A
7.   C

TEST 3

DIRECTIONS: Each question or incomplete statement is followed by several suggested answers or completions. Select the one that BEST answers the question or completes the statement. *PRINT THE LETTER OF THE CORRECT ANSWER IN THE SPACE AT THE RIGHT.*

Questions 1 -7.

DIRECTIONS: Questions 1 through 7 inclusive refer to the Tabulation of Turnstile Readings shown below, and to the note given beneath the tabulation. Refer to this tabulation and the note in answering these questions.

TABULATION OF TURNSTILE READINGS

Turnstile Number	TURNSTILE READINGS AT					
	5:30 A.M.	6:00 A.M.	7:00 A.M.	8:00 A.M.	9:00 A.M.	10:00 A.M.
1	45863	45872	45992	46348	46619	46756
2	89768	89789	89902	90713	91237	91285
3	89987	90006	90197	91312	91927	92011
4	18956	18963	19058	19561	19951	20000

NOTES: 1.   Turnstiles are operated by tokens costing $1.00 each.
   2.   The subway entrance at which these turnstiles are located is open, with a railroad clerk on duty, from 5:30 A.M. to 10:00 A.M.

1.   The number of passengers using turnstile No. 2 from 6:00 A.M. to 8:00 A.M. was

   A.   113   B.   713   C.   724   D.   924

1.____

2.   The *MOST* used turnstile from opening to closing was No.

   A.   1   B.   2   C.   3   D.   4

2.____

3.   The total number of passenger using turnstile No. 1 from opening to closing was

   A.   883   B.   893   C.   1883   D.   1893

3.____

4.   From 8:00 A.M. to 9:00 A.M. the railroad clerk sold exactly 800 tokens, while the turnstile readings for the four turnstiles show that a total of 1800 passengers passed through them in the same period. The number of passengers who purchased tokens was *MOST* probably

   A.   less than 800
   C.   between 800 and 1000
   B.   exactly 800
   D.   exactly 1800

4.____

5.   The cash taken in for the 800 tokens of question 4 was

   A. $160.00   B. $240.00   C. $300.00   D. $800.00

5.____

6. The number of passengers using turnstile No. 3 in the first half hour was   6._____

    A. 119   B. 81   C. 19   D. 9

7. The turnstile passing the *FEWEST* passengers from 9:00 A.M. to 10:00 A.M. was No.   7._____

    A. 1   B. 2   C. 3   D. 4

KEY (CORRECT ANSWERS)

    1. D
    2. C
    3. B
    4. A
    5. D
    6. C
    7. B

TEST 4

DIRECTIONS: Each question or incomplete statement is followed by several suggested answers or completions. Select the one that BEST answers the question or completes the statement. *PRINT THE LETTER OF THE CORRECT ANSWER IN THE SPACE AT THE RIGHT.*

Questions 1 -5.

DIRECTIONS: Questions 1 through 5 are based on the chart of HOURLY TURNSTILE READINGS shown below. Refer to this chart when answering these questions.

HOURLY TURNSTILE READINGS

| Turnstile | TURNSTILE READINGS AT | | | | |
Number	7:00 A.M.	8:00 A.M.	9:00 A.M.	10:00 A.M.	11:00 A.M.
1	37111	37905	38342	38451	38485
2	78432	79013	79152	79237	79306
3	45555	45921	45989	46143	46233
4	89954	90063	90121	90242	90299

1. The total number of passengers using turnstile No. 1 from 7:00 A.M. to 11:00 A.M. is   1.____

   A. 580   B. 794   C. 1374   D. 1594

2. The turnstile which registered the *LARGEST* number of fares from 7:00 A.M. to 8:00 M. is   2.____

   A. No. 1   B. No. 2   C. No. 3   D. No. 4

3. The total number of passengers using all four turnstiles between 10:00 A.M. and 11:00 A.M. is   3.____

   A. 57   B. 250   C. 396   D. 3271

4. Turnstile No. 4 registered the *HIGHEST* number of passengers between   4.____

   A.   7:00 A.M. and 8:00 A.M.   B.   9:00 A.M. and 10:00 A.M.
   C.   8:00 A.M. and 9:00 A.M.   D.   10:00 A.M. and 11:00 A.M.

5. The turnstile which registered the *LOWEST* number of passengers between 8:00 A.M. and 9:00 A.M. is   5.____

   A. No. 1   B. No. 2   C. No. 3   D. No. 4

KEY (CORRECT ANSWERS)

1. C
2. A
3. B
4. C
5. D

EXAMINATION SECTION
TEST 1

DIRECTIONS: Each question or incomplete statement is followed by several suggested answers or completions. Select the one that BEST answers the question or completes the statement. *PRINT THE LETTER OF THE CORRECT ANSWER IN THE SPACE AT THE RIGHT.*

Questions 1-8.

DIRECTIONS: Questions 1 through 8 are to be answered SOLELY on the Bulletin Order shown below. Refer to this Bulletin Order when answering these items.

BULLETIN ORDER NO. 9

Subject: Plugged Turnstiles   January 19, _____

Railroad clerks, especially those assigned to the midnight tour of duty, are again warned to be alert when a passenger reports that his token is stuck in a turnstile which will not let him through. If no platform man or gateman is available, take the passenger's name and address without leaving the booth, and request the passenger to pay an additional fare using one of the other turnstiles. Inform the passenger that the Authority will reimburse him for actual fare lost.

Railroad clerks are not to leave booths unattended in such instances, but will telephone the Station Department immediately.

Railroad clerks should notify the Transit Police Bureau immediately of any suspicious acts observed and are redirected to keep booth doors locked at all times. Booth doors must be closed and locked when railroad clerks are taking turnstile readings or retrieving tokens.

John Doe,
Superintendent

1. When a passenger reports a stuck turnstile, the railroad clerk should telephone the   1.____

   A. Superintendent   B. Authority
   C. Transit Police Bureau   D. Station Department

2. The total number of times that the title *railroad clerks* appears in the entire bulletin is   2.____

   A. 3   B. 4   C. 5   D. 6

3. When a passenger reports that a token is stuck in a turnstile, the railroad clerk should   3.____

   A. notify the Transit Police immediately
   B. tell the passenger to look for a gateman
   C. lock his booth and inspect the turnstile
   D. take the passenger's name and address

4. A passenger who properly reports the loss of a token in a plugged turnstile will PROBA-   4._____
    BLY be reimbursed through

    A. a special messenger   B. the railroad clerk
    C. a gateman   D. the regular mail

5. Retrieving tokens, as used in this bulletin, MOST probably means   5._____

    A. taking out tokens which have been deposited in turnstiles
    B. picking up tokens which have dropped to the floor
    C. paying out cash for tokens returned by passengers
    D. counting the number of tokens sold since the previous count

6. If railroad clerks at a certain location work in three consecutive 8-hour tours to cover the   6._____
    24 hours in a day and the A.M. tour finishes at 3:00 P.M., the hours of work for the mid-
    night tour are MOST likely

    A. 12:00 midnight to 8:00 A.M.
    B. 11:00 P.M. to 7:00 A.M.
    C. 10:00 P.M. to 6:00 A.M.
    D. 9:00 P.M. to 5:00 A.M.

7. If Bulletin Order No. 1 was issued on January 2, bulletins are being issued at the rate of   7._____

    A. one a day   B. one a week
    C. one every two days   D. two a week

8. From the statements in this bulletin, it is clear that there MUST be   8._____

    A. gatemen on duty at every change booth
    B. telephones in all change booths
    C. suspicious characters around every station
    D. platform men always on duty

_____

KEY (CORRECT ANSWERS)

1.	D	6.	B
2.	B	7.	C
3.	D	8.	B
4.	D		
5.	A		

_____

TEST 2

DIRECTIONS: Each question or incomplete statement is followed by several suggested answers or completions. Select the one that BEST answers the question or completes the statement. *PRINT THE LETTER OF THE CORRECT ANSWER IN THE SPACE AT THE RIGHT.*

Questions 1-7.

DIRECTIONS: Questions 1 through 7 are to be answered on the basis of the PROCEDURE FOR INSPECTION, REPAIRS, OR ALTERATIONS TO LOW TURNSTILES given below. Refer to this procedure when answering these questions.

PROCEDURE FOR INSPECTION, REPAIRS, OR ALTERATIONS TO LOW TURNSTILES

When a maintainer arrives at a station to repair or inspect a turnstile, the railroad clerk and the maintainer together will take the register reading of the turnstile, and the railroad clerk will record the reading on Form TAA-G-458 before any work is begun.

When the work is completed and before the turnstile is opened for service, the railroad clerk and the maintainer together will again take the register reading. The railroad clerk will enter this second reading on Form TAA-G-458. The difference between the two readings, representing the number of test registrations made on that turnstile, will also be entered.

The turnstile maintainer shall make a report in duplicate on Form TAM-L27 showing the register readings before and after adjustment, and shall have the railroad clerk initial the readings as verification. If test operation is by observation of passengers entering through the turnstile just repaired, the number of such passengers shall be noted in the *Remarks* column. The turnstile maintainer shall also enter the time of start and finish of the work, and on the original copy of the report only, the type of inspection or work done.

The railroad clerk shall transmit the duplicate of Form TAM-L27 together with his Form TAA-G-458 to Audit of Passenger Revenue.

1. The number of entries on the maintainer's Form TAM-L27 that the railroad clerk is required to initial for each turnstile worked on is   1.____

   A. 1   B. 2   C. 3   D. 4

2. The number of entries that the railroad clerk is required to make on Form TAA-G-458 is   2.____

   A. 1   B. 2   C. 3   D. 4

3. In accordance with the foregoing, the number of copies of Form TAA-G-458 that MUST be made out by the railroad clerk is   3.____

   A. 4   B. 3   C. 2   D. 1

4. With respect to Form TAM-L27, the letters *TA* MOST likely stand for   4.____

   A. transit authority   B. token adjustment
   C. turnstile alteration   D. time account

5. The form of test operation specifically mentioned in the procedure is by   5.____

    A. use of special counters
    B. observation of passengers entering
    C. use of a stated number of tokens
    D. changing the register reading

6. It is stated in the procedure that the maintainer should enter in the *Remarks* column of   6.____
    Form TAM-L27 the

    A. initial register reading
    B. number of test registrations
    C. number of passengers involved in test registrations
    D. final register reading

7. The information that is NOT included when the railroad clerk transmits the two forms to   7.____
    Audit of Passenger Revenue is the

    A. final turnstile reading
    B. type of work done
    C. number of test registrations
    D. number of test operations made by passengers entering

———————

KEY (CORRECT ANSWERS)

1.	B		6.	C
2.	C		7.	B
3.	D			
4.	A			
5.	B			

———————

TEST 3

DIRECTIONS: Each question or incomplete statement is followed by several suggested answers or completions. Select the one that BEST answers the question or completes the Statement. *PRINT THE LETTER OF THE CORRECT ANSWER IN THE SPACE AT THE RIGHT.*

Questions 1-8.

DIRECTIONS: Questions 1 through 8 are to be answered on the basis of the following paragraphs about accident statistics. Read these statistics carefully before answering these questions.

ACCIDENT STATISTICS

Accidents are among our nation's leading killers, maulers, and money wasters. In the United States during 1998, according to the National Safety Council figures, there were 100,000 fatal accidents of all kinds, and ten million various types of disabling injuries. Some 40,000 deaths involved motor vehicles. The home accounted for 29,000 fatalities, and public places 17,000. There were 14,000 deaths and two million disabling injuries in industry.

In 1998, the total cost of accidents in the United States was at least 16 billion dollars. For industry alone, the cost of accidents was 5 billion dollars, equal to $70 per worker. The total time lost was about 230 million man days of work.

1. The statistics quoted above are for   1.____

    A. the home *only*   B. the entire United States
    C. New York State   D. New York City

2. The statistics quoted above are for the year   2.____

    A. 1995   B. 1996   C. 1997   D. 1998

3. Of the 100,000 fatal accidents of all kinds, those NOT involved with motor vehicles totaled   3.____

    A. 17,000   B. 29,000   C. 40,000   D. 60,000

4. The number of disabling injuries of all kinds which were listed for industry was _____ million.   4.____

    A. 10   B. 8   C. 4   D. 2

5. Accidents cost our nation AT LEAST _____ dollars.   5.____

    A. 16 billion   B. 5 billion
    C. 10 million   D. 2 million

6. The number of deaths due to accidents in the home was close to   6.____

    A. 15,000   B. 20,000   C. 30,000   D. 40,000

7. The number of deaths per day from accidents of all kinds averaged about   7.____

    A. 275   B. 300   C. 325   D. 350

8. During the year for which these statistics are given, the cost of industrial accidents per   8.____
   worker was

   A. $230   B. $70   C. $17   D. $5

_____

KEY (CORRECT ANSWERS)

1.	B		6.	C
2.	D		7.	A
3.	D		8.	B
4.	D			
5.	A			

_____

TEST 4

DIRECTIONS: Each question or incomplete statement is followed by several suggested answers or completions. Select the one that BEST answers the question or completes the statement. *PRINT THE LETTER OF THE CORRECT ANSWER IN THE SPACE AT THE RIGHT.*

Questions 1-6.

DIRECTIONS: Questions 1 through 6 are to be answered on the basis of the Bulletin Order given below. Refer to this Bulletin Order when answering these questions.

BULLETIN ORDER NO. 67

Subject: Procedure for Handling Fire Occurrences   6-17-_____

In order that the Fire Department may be notified of all fires, even those that have been extinguished by our own employees, any employee having knowledge of a fire must notify the Station Department Office immediately on telephone extensions: D-4177, D-4181, D-4185, or D-4189.

Specific information regarding the fire should include the location of the fire, the approximate distance north or south of the nearest station, and the track designation, line and division.

In addition, the report should contain information as to the status of the fire and whether our forces have extinguished it or if Fire Department equipment is needed.

When all information has been obtained, the Station Supervisor in charge in the Station Department Office will notify the Desk Trainmaster of the division involved.

Richard Roe,
Superintendent

1. An employee having knowledge of a fire should FIRST notify the   1.____

    A. Station Department Office   B. Fire Department
    C. Desk Trainmaster   D. Station Supervisor

2. If Bulletin Order No. 1 was issued on January 2, bulletins are being issued at the monthly   2.____
    average of

    A. 8   B. 10   C. 12   D. 14

3. It is clear from the bulletin that   3.____

    A. employees are expected to be expert fire fighters
    B. many fires occur on the transit system
    C. train service is usually suspended whenever a fire occurs
    D. some fires are extinguished without the help of the Fire Department

4. From the information furnished in this bulletin, it can be assumed that the   4._____

    A. Station Department Office handles a considerable number of telephone calls
    B. Superintendent investigates the handling of all subway fires
    C. Fire Department is notified only in case of large fires
    D. employee first having knowledge of the fire must call all 4 extensions

5. The PROBABLE reason for notifying the Fire Department even when the fire has been   5._____
extinguished by a subway employee is because the Fire Department is

    A. a city agency
    B. still responsible to check the fire
    C. concerned with fire prevention
    D. required to clean up after the fire

6. Information about the fire NOT specifically required is   6._____

    A. track   B. time of day
    C. station   D. division

———————

KEY (CORRECT ANSWERS)

1.	A		4.	A
2.	C		5.	C
3.	D		6.	B

———————

TEST 5

DIRECTIONS: Each question or incomplete statement is followed by several suggested answers or completions. Select the one that BEST answers the question or completes the statement. *PRINT THE LETTER OF THE CORRECT ANSWER IN THE SPACE AT THE RIGHT.*

Questions 1-4.

DIRECTIONS: Questions 1 through 4 are to be answered on the basis of the REGULATIONS RELATING TO VOTING ON PRIMARY DAY as given below. Read these regulations carefully before answering these questions.

REGULATIONS RELATING TO VOTING ON PRIMARY DAY

The polls are open from 3:00 to 10:00 P.M. Employees who are on duty Primary Day during the period polls are open, and who would not have two consecutive hours free time to vote, will be granted leave of absence for two hours without loss of pay.

Examples:

1. Employees reporting for work at 3 PM to and including 4:59 PM will be allowed two hours leave with pay.
2. Employees who report to work at 5 PM or thereafter, no time to be allowed.
3. Employees who complete their tour of duty and are cleared on or before 8 PM, no time to be allowed.

1. A two-hour leave of absence with pay will be granted to employees who are on duty Primary Day if they   1.____

   A. have to work two hours while the polls are open
   B. would not have two consecutive hours free time to vote
   C. are working a day tour
   D. are working a night tour

2. An employee working an evening tour will be allowed two hours with pay if he has to report for work at _____ PM.   2.____

   A. 3:00   B. 5:00   C. 7:00   D. 9:00

3. An employee working an afternoon tour will be allowed two hours with pay if he clears at _____ PM.   3.____

   A. 6:00   B. 7:00   C. 8:00   D. 9:00

4. An employee working an afternoon tour will NOT be allowed any time off if he clears at _____ PM.   4.____

   A. 8:00   B. 8:30   C. 9:30   D. 10:00

KEY (CORRECT ANSWERS)

1. B
2. A
3. D
4. A

———

EXAMINATION SECTION

TEST 1

DIRECTIONS: Each question or incomplete statement is followed by several suggested answers or completions. Select the one that BEST answers the question or completes the statement. *PRINT THE LETTER OF THE CORRECT ANSWER IN THE SPACE AT THE RIGHT.*

Questions 1-7.

DIRECTIONS: Questions 1 through 7 are to be answered SOLELY on the basis of the information given in the paragraph below and the Visitor's Release form.

On Friday, December 19, at 9:15 A.M., Joan Sanford, who represented the Adam Hart Manufacturing Company, appeared at the Property Protection Agent booth at the 207th Street, Manhattan, Main Shop. She stated that she wanted to see Superintendent Patterson about a parts contract with her firm, which makes spare parts for subway cars. The Agent called Mr. Patterson, who said he expected her. The Agent thereupon asked her to complete a Visitor's Release form, which she did. O the form she indicated her age as 27, her occupation as salesperson, her supervisor's name as Lawrence Austin, the firm's location at 1427 Cedar St., Glendale, N.Y., and her home address as 25-16 65th Road, Oak Point, N.Y. Agent Paul Jones signed the Visitor's Release form as witness to her signature. She then entered the facility and left Transit Authority property at 2 P.M., at which time Mr. Jones gave Miss Sanford a copy of the Visitor's Release form.

TRANSIT AUTHORITY
VISITOR'S RELEASE

The undersigned hereby agrees to hold harmless and indemnify The City of New York, Metropolitan Transportation Authority, New York City Transit Authority, and their respective members, officers, agents, and employees, from any and all loss and liability for damages on account of injuries (including death) to persons and damage to property attributable in whole or in part to the negligence of the undersigned while on or about the premises of the New York City Transit Authority.

NYCTA Location to be Visited:_____(1)_____
Duration of Visit: From _____A.M. _____P.M. _____
　　　　　　　　　To _____A.M. _____P.M. _____(2)
Reason for Visit:_____(3)_____
Age:_(4)___ Occupation: _____(5)_____
Firm Represented:_____(6)_____
Employer: _____(7)_____
Address of Firm: _____(8)_____
Dated: ____(9)___ (Signed)_____(10)_____
　　　　　Address:_____(11)_____
Witness: _____(12)_____

1.   Which of the following should be on Line 4?   1.____
      A. 2 P.M.   B. 57
      C. 107th St. Shop   D. 27

2.   Which of the following should be on Line 6?   2.____
      A. Joan Sanford   B. Adam Hart Manufacturing Co.
      C. Oak Point Associates   D. Patterson Manufacturing Co.

3.   Which of the following should be on Line 11?   3.____
      A. 1427 Cedar St., Glendale, N.Y.
      B. 25-16 65th Road, Oak Point, N.Y.
      C. 3961 Tenth Avenue, Manhattan, at 207th St.
      D. 26-15 65th Ave., Oak Point, N.Y.

4.   Which of the following should be on Line 12?   4.____
      A. Miss Sanford's signature   B. Mr. Patterson's signature
      C. Paul Jones' signature   D. Lawrence Austin's name

5.   On which of the following lines should *1327 Cedar St., Glendale, N.Y.* be   5.____
      entered?
      A. 2   B. 3   C. 7   D. 8

6.   What is Miss Sanford's occupation?   6.____
      A. Superintendent   B. Protection Agent
      C. Salesperson   D. Manager, Sales

7.   Which of the following should be entered in Section 2 of the form?   7.____
      A. 9:00; 2:00   B. 9:15; 2:00   C. 9:15; 2:15   D. 9:15; 3:00

Questions 8-17.

DIRECTIONS: Questions 8 through 17 are to be answered SOLELY on the basis of the
               following paragraphs titled SCRAP TRANSFER and the Record of Scrap
               Award Form.

Protection Agent Robert Green, Pass No. 104123, was assigned to Post 27A at the main entrance of the Fifth Ave. Brooklyn Train Yard on Thursday, October 23 on the 8 A.M.-to-4 P.M. tour. At 10:10 A.M., a scrap removal truck, No. 64, license plate AB-4126, from the J.H. Trucking Company stopped at the gate. The driver showed Agent Green a scrap contract with Award No. 1626 for the removal of 12 headlamps from this location.

Agent Green called Supervisor Raymond Hadley in Storeroom 18 for verification of the award. Supervisor Hadley verified the award. The driver then proceeded to Storeroom 18, where he loaded the headlamps into the truck. Hadley then made out a Materials Permit, signed it, and placed his pass number (521800) on it, and gave it to the driver. At the gate, the driver presented the Materials Permit to Agent Green, who logged out the truck at 10:40 A.M., whereupon the truck left for its destination in the Bronx.

Agent Green transcribed the information on his registry sheet and the Materials Permit to a Record of Scrap Award form, which he handed to Line Supervisor Brian Sullivan (Pass No. 756349), who had just arrived at the post. Line Supervisor Sullivan, after having checked the form carefully, signed it and wrote his pass number on it.

RECORD OF SCRAP AWARD

Date_____(1)____

Post No._____(2)_____   Tour_____(3)____

Name of Carrier_____(4)_____   Award No.___(5)__

Truck License No._____(6)_____

Truck No._____(7)_____

Destination:_____

Time In:_____(9)_____   Time Out:_____(10)_____

Description of Scrap:_____(11)_____

Amount:_____(12)_____

Name of Supervisor or Designee:_____(13)_____

Pass No._____

_____(14)_____   ___(15)_____
TRANSIT PROPERTY PROTECTION AGENT   PASS NO.

_____(16)_____   ___(17)_____
LINE SUPERVISOR SIGNATURE   PASS NO.

8. Which of the following should be on Line 2?   8.____
    A. 27A   B. Coney Island
    C. Storeroom 18   D. Main Gate

9. Which of the following should be on Line 3?   9.____
    A. 12 Midnight – 8 A.M.   B. 12 P.M. – 8 P.M.
    C. 8 A.M. – 4 P.M.   D. 4 P.M. – 12 P.M.

10. Which of the following should be on Line 4?   10.____
    A. J.H. Trucking Co.   B. Line Supervisor Sullivan
    C. Transit Authority   D. Storeroom 18

11. Which of the following should be on Line 8?   11.____
    A. Fifth Ave. Yard   B. Bronx, N.Y.
    C. Storeroom 18   D. Post 27A

12. Which of the following should be on Line 10?   12.____
    A. 9:10 A.M.   B. 10:10 A.M.   C. 10:30 A.M.   D. 10:40 A.M.

13. Which of the following should be on Line 16? _____ signature. 13.____
    A. Robert Green's   B. Brian Sullivan's
    C. the truck driver's   D. Raymond Hadley's

14. On which of the following lines should *104123* be entered?   14.____
    A. 10   B. 12   C. 15   D. 17

15. On which of the following lines should *AB4216* be entered?   15.____
    A. 1   B. 3   C. 6   D. 13

16. On which of the following lines should *12 headlamps* be entered?   16.____
    A. 3   B. 11   C. 14   D. 17

17. On which of the following lines should *10:10 A.M.* be entered?   17.____
    A. 8   B. 9   C. 10   D. 11

Questions 18-22.

DIRECTIONS: Questions 18 through 22 are to be answered SOLELY on the basis of the information in the KEY STATIONS DIRECTORY below. Key Stations are locations which Protection Agents must visit and inspect on their hourly rounds.

KEY STATIONS DIRECTORY

Key Station No.
1   Protection Agent's booth at Flushing Train Yard
2   On parking lot fence adjacent to No. 4 track
3   On stairwell No. 8 in the Boiler Room
4   On the door leading to the second floor men's locker room
5   Alongside the soda machine in the second floor lunchroom
6   On the oilhouse door
7   Alongside the bulletin board in the main shop
8   Next to fire extinguisher No. 12 on the wall to the left of the entrance to the Supervisor's Office
9   On the bumper block of Track No. 10

18. The number of the key station near the main shop bulletin board is   18.____
    A. 5   B. 6   C. 7   D. 8

19. Where is Key Station No. 4?   19.____
    A. On the parking lot fence adjacent to Track 4
    B. On the door of the second floor men's locker room
    C. On the oilhouse door
    D. In the second floor lunchroom

20. The number of the key station in the Protection Agent's booth is   20.____
    A. 1   B. 3   C. 7   D. 9

21. No. 5 key station is located   21.____
    A. next to fire extinguisher No. 6 in the Protection Agent's booth
    B. on the bumper block of Track 10
    C. in the second floor lunchroom next to the soda machine
    D. on the parking lot fence near Track No. 4

22. The number of the key station on the parking lot fence adjacent to Track No. 4 is

    A. 1   B. 2   C. 3   D. 8

22.____

Questions 23-25.

DIRECTIONS: Questions 23 through 25 are to be answered SOLELY on the basis of the information contained in the following instructions on FIRST AID KITS.

FIRST AID KITS

First aid kits will be used only in case of injury to employees or passengers. A <u>Report of Use of First Aid Kit</u> form will be prepared in triplicate and forwarded to the Station Department Office whenever the seal of the kit is broken, regardless of whether any of the contents is used.

After use, the kit will be temporarily resealed with a shurlock seal bearing the impress of the booth punch. An outside tag will be attached to the seal with the following information on the back of the tag.

Opened:_____A.M./P.M.   _____
           (Time)   (Date)
By:_____
        (Name)   (Title)   (Pass No.)
Resealed:_____A.M./P.M. _____
          (Time)   (Date)
By:_____
        (Name)   (Title)   (Pass No.)

Upon receipt of <u>Report of use of First Aid Kit</u> form, the P.M. Station Supervisor will arrange to replace the items used and reseal the kit, using a special seal pouch.

23. First aid kits may be used whenever
    A. the seal of the kit is broken
    B. the Station Supervisor approves
    C. their contents have to be checked
    D. there is an injury to employees or passengers

23.____

24. Who should arrange for the replacement of the items used in a first aid kit?
    A. Station Agent   B. Cleaner
    C. Station Supervisor   D. Employee who used the kit

24.____

25. The information written on the back of the tag attached to the first aid kit should contain the
    A. social security number of the person who opened the kit
    B. pass number of the person who resealed the kit
    C. time when the accident took place
    D. place where the accident happened

25.____

KEY (CORRECT ANSWERS)

1.	D		11.	B/C
2.	B		12.	D
3.	B		13.	B
4.	C		14.	C
5.	D		15.	C
6.	C		16.	B
7.	B		17.	B
8.	A		18.	C
9.	C		19.	B
10.	A		20.	A

21.	C
22.	B
23.	D
24.	C
25.	B

———————

TEST 2

DIRECTIONS: Each question or incomplete statement is followed by several suggested answers or completions. Select the one that BEST answers the question or completes the statement. *PRINT THE LETTER OF THE CORRECT ANSWER IN THE SPACE AT THE RIGHT.*

Questions 1-6.

DIRECTIONS: Questions 1 through 6 are to be answered SOLELY on the basis of the information contained in the CLEANING REPORT BELOW.

CLEANING REPORT

To: Cleaner (TA) <u>J. Brown</u>, Badge No. <u>3461</u>, Pass No. <u>327351</u>

The following cleaning report must be filled out by you and handed in before you go off duty. Part I shall be prepared by a Station Supervisor, Assistant Station Supervisor, Railroad Clerk, or Claim Investigator. Part II must then be filled out by you.

PART I
This part must be filled in by Station Supervisor, Assistant Station Supervisor, Railroad Clerk, or Claim Investigator before second part is completed by Cleaner (TA).

Date of Accident: *Feb. 17*, Time: *11:20* A.M./P.M. Line: *(A)* , Station: *34th Street*, Exact Location: *Stairway S-6* Name of Injured: *Gregory Peckham* Address: *124 W. 16th St., N.Y.,N.Y.* Accident occurred before/while/after *John Brown* Title: *Cleaner (TA)* Pass No.: *327751* came on duty/was on duty/went off duty.

PART II
This part must be completed and all questions answered by the above Cleaner but only after Part I has been filled in. I *John Brown*, Pass No. *327751* was on duty at the *34th St.* Station on *Feb. 27* from *8:00* A.M./P.M. to *4:00* A.M./P.M. Upon my arrival at the station, I proceeded to inspect and then clean the entire station including *Stairway S-6* and left it *in good condition*. I swept and cleaned that part of the station at about *11:00* A.M./P.M., the same as I do on every tour of duty and cleaned and inspected it again at about *2:00* A.M./P.M. before I went off duty. Did you inspect scene after accident? *Yes* If you did so, give time and condition.
Date: *Feb. 27* Time: *11:45* A.M./P.M. Condition: *Clean and in good condition*
Weather Conditions *Clear*
Was there any snow or ice on the street surface? *No*
Was there any snow or ice on the part of the station involved in accident? *No*
Were there any defects or obstructions at place of accident? *No*
REMARKS: (Here give details as to conditions existing and all you know about this accident.
I saw a passenger lose his balance while descending Stairway S-6 and fall down the steps. He bruised his face. I inspected the stairway at 11:45 A.M. and found it clean and in good condition.
Did you see the accident? *Yes*
Date report was signed by you: *Feb. 27*
FULL NAME: *John Brown* ADDRESS: *154 E. 18th St., N.Y., N.Y., Apt. 3C*

1. The accident occurred on   1.____
   A. Stairway N-6   B. Northbound platform
   C. Southbound platform   D. Stairway S-6

2. The stairway where the accident occurred was cleaned at   2.____
   A. 8:00 A.M.   B. 11:00 A.M.   C. 11:45 A.M.   D. 4:00 P.M.

3. Part I of the Cleaning Report may be filled out by any of the following   3.____
   employees EXCEPT the
   A. Station Supervisor   B. Cleaner
   C. Railroad Clerk   D. Claim Investigator

4. The accident to the passenger took place at   4.____
   A. 11:00 A.M.   B. 11:30 A.M.   C. 11:45 P.M.   D. 2:00 P.M.

5. Part II of the Cleaning Report was made out by the   5.____
   A. Assistant Station Supervisor   B. Station Supervisor
   C. Cleaner   D. Railroad Clerk

6. What was the pass number of the Cleaner?   6.____
   A. 323751   B. 372351   C. 327351   D. 327531

Question 7.

DIRECTIONS: Question 7 is to be answered SOLELY on the basis of the following information
and the chart which appears on the following page.

As a supervisor, you have assigned Police Communications Technician Newhardt to work
ERS for the day. During the tour, he received the calls listed below:

1. Spanish assist
2. Report of a fire at 366 East 66th Street, Apt. 9
3. Request for the 14th Precinct's address and telephone number
4. Request for an ambulance for an E.D.P. in front of 1717 Broadway
5. Fire Department test call
6. Series of tapping (2-3) from ERS box 2514

Near the end of the tour (1520 hours), you inspect his ERS log, and you notice that he has
failed to complete certain information.

EMERGENCY REPORTING SYSTEM LOG

DATE: _March 21_   BOROUGH: _Manhattan_
TOUR: _0800 x 1600_   POSITION: _POS 10_

	A	B	C	D	E	F	G	H	I	J	K	L	M	N
						TYPE OF CALL								
	TIME	BOX #	CPR#	PRAU	INFO	TEST	NA	MISC	INPUT	JOB #	CODE SIGNALS	INCIDENT LOCATION	EMP ASS.	FINAL DISP
1	1430	3691	001					✓				Referred to Spanish		
2	1436	4266	001							52611		366 E. 66 St.	23A	91
3	1439		001											
4	1445		001									1717 Broadway	34B	90Z
5		4444	001											
6	1449	2514	001						✓				26A	93C
4														
8														
9														
10														
11														
12														
13														
14														
15														
16		TOTALS									VERIFIED BY _____ SUPERVISOR'S SIGNATURE			

7. Which of the following series of letters and numbers represents information omitted in the log?   7.____
    A. A5, B4, J5, M1, G16, D16, I4, F16, E3, J6, K2, G7, M4, N6, B2, L1, M2, I1, I16
    B. A5, B4, E4, K9, J6, M6, L1, M2, B5, L3, I5, C6, B3, L6, M6, L5, G6, I16
    C. A5, B4, J5, K4, E3, G5, K6, I4, I2, K2, K6, D16, B2, L1, M2, I1, G6, I16
    D. A5, B3, B4, E3, F5, J4, K2, K4, J6, K6, L6, E16, F16, H16, I16, I4, I2, D16, G16

8. Assume that the Spring system fails and all Bronx operators are told by Supervising Dispatcher Shelton that a Backup Slip Operation will be in effect. Police Communications Technician Jordan then receives a call over the Emergency Reporting System indicating a call from fire box 7215. A Mrs. Smith is on the line reporting a heavy smoke condition in her third floor hallway at 6773 Dayton Drive. Operator Jordan disengages the call with Mrs. Smith and proceeds to connect to the Bronx fire operator. Fire Operator 737 accepts the information and advises Operator Jordan that a unit will be sent, although there have been numerous unfounded alarms at this location in the past. Operator Jordan then gives the slip to Supervising Dispatcher Shelton, who is passing by her position. The slip is shown on the following page.   8.____

After checking the slip, Supervising Dispatcher Shelton should return it to Operator Jordan and tell her that she omitted the

A. caller's name, routing, fire box number, time, precinct
B. fire box number, caller's name, fire operator's number, time
C. fire operator's number, fire box number, sector, date
D. fire box number, precinct, intersection, time

Questions 9-10.

DIRECTIONS: Questions 9 and 10 are to be answered SOLELY on the basis of the following information.

Police Communications Technicians must be able to identify and assign codes to the crimes described in the calls they receive. All crimes are coded by number and by priority. The priority code number indicates the seriousness of the crime. The lower the priority number, the more serious the crime.

Listed below is a chart of several crimes and their definitions. The corresponding crime code and priority code number are given.

CRIME	DEFINITION	CRIME CODE	PRIORITY CODE
Criminal Mischief	Occurs when a person intentionally damages another person's property	29	6
Harrassment	Occurs when a person intentionally annoys another person by striking, shoving, or kicking them without causing injury	27	8
Aggravated Harrassment	Occurs when a person intentionally annoys another person by using any form of communication	28	9
Theft of Service	Occurs when a person intentionally avoids payment for services given	25	7

9. Communications Technician Rogers received a call from Mrs. Freeman, who stated that her next door neighbor, whom she had an argument with, has thrown a rock through her apartment window. Which one of the following is the CORRECT crime code?

9.____

    A. 29   B. 28   C. 27   D. 25

10. Communications Technician Tucker received a call from a man who stated that he is a waiter at the Frontier Diner. He states that one of his customers was refusing to pay for his meal. Which one of the following is the CORRECT priority code number for this crime?

10.____

    A. 6   B. 7   C. 8   D. 9

Question 11.

DIRECTIONS: Question 11 is to be answered SOLELY on the basis of the information below and the form appearing on the following page

Election of Rate of Charge Against Annual and/or Sick Leave Balances
for Absence Due to Injury Sustained in the Performance of Official Duties

(Pursuant to Regulation 7.0 of the Leave Regulations for Employees Who are
Under the Career and Salary Plan)

> INSTRUCTIONS: The injured employee, or an authorized person acting in his behalf, should submit this election notice (in duplicate) to the head of his department or agency within the first seven calendar days of absence due to injury sustained in the performance of official duties.

I, _____, employed in _____
      (Print name of injured employee)   (Print name of city department or agency)
in a position which is subject to the Leave Regulations for employees who are under the Career and Salary Plan, or any authorized agent, do hereby elect the option designated below, subject to the conditions attached thereto, as the one to be applied in determining the charge, if any, to be made against my annual and/or sick leave balances for absence due to injury sustained in the performance of my official duties.
(Check one option only)

    OPTION I: I elect to receive the difference between the amount of my weekly salary and the compensation rate, subject to the following conditions:

    (a)   A pro-rated charge shall be made against my sick leave and/or annual leave balances equal to the number of working days of absence less the number of working days represented by the Worker's Compensation payments, and;

    (b)   My accrued sick leave and/or annual leave balances, or such leave credits advanced to me in accordance with the Career and Salary Plan Leave Regulations, are adequate to meet the charges made against them for supplementary pay, and;

    (c)   The injury sustained by me was not the result of my willful gross disobedience of safety rules or my willful failure to use a safety device, nor was I under the influence of alcohol or narcotics at the time of injury, nor did I willfully intend to bring about injury or death upon myself or another, and;

(d) Such medical examinations will be undergone by me as are requested by the Worker's Compensation Division of the Law Department and my agency, and when found fit for duty by said physicians, I shall return to my employment.

OPTION 2: I elect to receive Workmen's Compensation benefits in their entirety with no charge against sick leave and/or annual leave.

Injured Employee's Signature		Date
This shaded section should be completed only if the injured employee cannot sign and must designate an authorized person to sign in his behalf	Authorized designer's (print)	Relationship to injured employee
	Authorized designer's address	
	Authorized designer's signature	Date
	Witness' name (print)	
	Witness' address	
	Witness' signature	Date

Employing Department should forward duplicate copy to Worker's Compensation Division of Law Department

11. Lt. Perry is reviewing a DP2002 form (see the form on the previous page) that was prepared as a result of an agent's on-the-job injury. Which one of the following statements concerning this form is CORRECT?   11.____

A. If all of the agent's sick leave and annual leave have been used up, only Option 1 may be selected.
B. The person who signs as a witness must have seen the accident and must be willing to swear that the agent was not at fault.
C. If the agent wishes to switch from Option 1 to Option 2 when sick leave and annual leave have been used up, both Option 1 and Option 2 should be checked.
D. An agent with sufficient sick leave and annual leave who wishes to continue receiving a regular paycheck should choose Option 1.

Question 12.

DIRECTIONS: Question 12 is to be answered SOLELY on the basis of the following form.

EMPLOYEE'S NOTICE OF INJURY

ANSWER ALL QUESTIONS FULLY. THIS IS YOUR NOTICE TO YOUR EMPLOYER OF INJURY ON THE JOB. PRINT OR WRITE LEGIBLY.

Full name of injured person *Mary*   *M*   *Doe*
          (First)   (Middle)   (Last)
Address   *110 Finkel Road*
Employee's S.S. No.   *172-00-1001*   Date of Birth   *10/20/60*
Name of employer   CITY OF NEW YORK – DEPARTMENT OF *Transportation*
Date of accident   *5/6/15*   Hour *10:15* A.M.   P.M.
Exact location where accident happened *1ˢᵗ Ave and E. 57ᵗʰ St. Northwest Corner*

How did accident happen? (Describe fully) *While walking on 1ˢᵗ Ave. and E. 57ᵗʰ St., I stepped into a pothole, fell, and sprained my right ankle and my left wrist*

Nature and extent of injury *Sprained left ankle and left wrist*

Did you inform your superior of this accident?   *Yes*   Date *5/6/15*
Name such person   *Lt. Fudd*
Names and addresses of witnesses *Lt. Fudd   182 Mulholland Dr., N.Y. 11726*

Date *5/6/15*   (Sign here)   *Mary Doe*
          THIS IS NOT A CLAIM FORM. A CLAIM FORM MAYH BE SECURED AT
          ANY OFFICE OF THE STATE WORKER'S COMPENSATION BOARD

12.   On May 6, Traffic Enforcement Agent Mary M. Doe, SS# 172-00-1001, had an accident at 10:15 A.M. while patrolling her sector. She was walking south on the east side of 1ˢᵗ Avenue and was about to cross East 57ᵗʰ Street when she tripped on a pothole and fell, spraining her right ankle and left wrist. Lt. Fudd was on the scene at the time and witnessed the accident. After the agent received medical attention, Lt. Fudd reviews the Employee's Notice of Injury form shown on the previous page, including the reports of the

    I.   Description of the injury
    II.   Date and time of the accident
    III.   Location where the accident occurred
    IV.   Employee's Social Security number

Which of the above entries are correct and which are incorrect?
_____ are correct, but _____ are incorrect.

    A. I and II; III and IV   B. I and III; II and IV
    C. II and IV; I and III   D. III and IV; I and II

12.____

Question 13.

DIRECTIONS: Question 13 is to be answered SOLELY on the basis of the form which is shown below.

DEPT. OF TRANSPORTATION
TRAFFIC CONTROL DIVISION-ENFORCEMENT
DAILY FIELD PATROL SHEET

MULTIPLE PAGE CHECK	
PAGE	OF

I - AGENT IDENTIFICATION INFORMATION

NAME			RANK	BADGE NO.
Jones, Alice			TEA 1	007

PRE=PRINTED ADHESIVE LABEL TO BE ATTACHED HERE BY LT. OR INDIVIDUAL AGENT

TAX REG NO	CMD	ENF GRP	SQD	MO.	DAY	YR
235719	6Q3	F7P	G	05	30	15

II - MISCELLANEOUS INFORMATION

POST or SECTOR	POST CHANGE
6301	

MEAL	VEHICLE NO.	PORTABLE NO.
1100	-	666

III - TIME & ATTENDANCE

REGULAR TOUR		OVERTIME TOUR		TOTAL HOURS	ROO
FROM	TO	FROM	TO		
07:00	03:00			08:00	X

IV - DETAILED ACTIVITIES

ACTIVITY DESCRIPTION	TOW VOUCHER NO.	ACTIVITY CODE	TIME ARRIVED	TIME DEPARTED	POST CODE	SUMS ISSD	TOWS
DO		DOAD	7:00	07:15			
TRAVEL		TRVL	07:15	08:00			
On 7 Av from 3 St TO 8 St		ISSP	08:00	09:00	6301	8	
PERSONAL		PR5N	09:00	09:15			
On 7 Av from 3 St TO 8 St		ISSP	09:15	11:00	6301	12	
MEAL		MEAL	11:00	12:45			
On 7 Av from 3 St TO 8 St		ISSP	12:45	01:30	6301	8	
TRAVEL		TRVL	01:30	02:15			
DO		DOAD	02:15	03:00			
	TOTAL SUMMONSES ISSUED/VEHICLES TOWED					28	

VII - SPECIAL SUMMONS ACTIVITIES

POST CODE	COMLO	MISC 1	MISC 2	MISC 3	MISC 4
TOTAL					

V - SUMMONSES USED

STARTING SUMMONS NO.	ENDING SUMMONS NO.	TOTAL
978676763	97867706	25
978677015	978677033	3
		28

VIII - SIGNATURES

AGENT	Alice Jones
LL	Thomas Smart
LL	

TIME/DATE STAMP TO FIELD	TIME/DATE STAMP FROM FIELD

VI – ERROR SUMMONSES & MOVING VIOLATIONS

TYPE	CODE	SUMMONS NO.
E	E	97867742

13. Lt. Howard is reviewing Traffic Enforcement Agent Jones' Daily Field Patrol   13.____
    Sheet (TCD-210), the front side of which is shown on the preceding page. The
    Lieutenant checks the following entries:
        I.   Activity Codes
        II.   Summonses Used
        III. Signatures
        IV. Post Codes
        V.   Time and Attendance
    The Lieutenant should notice that there are errors in _____, but not in _____.
    A. I and IV; II, III, and V   B. II and III; I, IV, and V
    C. II and V; I, III, and IV   D. I, III, and V; II and IV

Questions 14-20.

DIRECTIONS: Questions 14 through 20 are to be answered SOLELY on the basis of the
                    numbered boxes on the Arrest Report and paragraph below.

ARREST REPORT

1. Arrest Number	2. Precinct of Arrest		3. Date/Time of Arrest		4. Defendant's Name	5. Defendant's Address
6. Defendant's Date of Birth	7. Sex	8. Race	9. Height	10. Weight	11. Location of Arrest	12. Date & Time of Occurrence
13. Location of Occurrence	14. Complaint Number		15. Victim's Name	16. Victim's Address		17. Victim's Date of Birth
18. Precinct of Complaint	19. Arresting Officer's Name		20. Shield Number		21. Assigned Unit Precinct	22. Date of Complaint

On Friday, December 13, at 11:45 P.M., while leaving a store at 235 Spring Street, Grace O'Connell, a white female, 5'2", 130 lbs., was approached by a white male, 5'11", 200 lbs., who demanded her money and jewelry. As the man ran and turned down River Street, Police Officer William James, Shield Number 31724, assigned to the 14th Precinct, gave chase and apprehended him in front of 523 River Street. The prisoner, Gerald Grande, who resides at 17 Water Street, was arrested at 12:05 A.M., was charged with robbery, and taken to the 13th Precinct, where he was assigned Arrest Number 53048. Miss O'Connell, who resides at 275 Spring St., was given Complaint Number 82460.

14. On the basis of the Arrest Report and paragraph above, the CORRECT entry   14.____
    for Box Number 3 should be
    A. 11:45 P.M., 12/13   B. 11:45 P.M., 12/14
    C. 12:05 A.M., 12/13   D. 12:05 A.M., 12/14

15. On the basis of the Arrest Report and paragraph above, the CORRECT entry   15.____
    for Box Number 21 should be
    A. 13th Precinct   B. 14th Precinct
    C. Mounted Unit   D. 32nd Precinct

16. On the basis of the Arrest Report and paragraph above, the CORRECT entry for Box Number 11 should be
    A. 235 Spring St.
    C. 275 Spring St.
    B. 523 River St.
    D. 17 Water St.

16.____

17. On the basis of the Arrest Report and paragraph above, the CORRECT entry for Box Number 2 should be
    A. 13th Precinct
    C. Mounted Unit
    B. 14th Precinct
    D. 32nd Precinct

17.____

18. On the basis of the Arrest Report and paragraph above, the CORRECT entry for Box Number 13 should be
    A. 523 River St.
    C. 275 Spring St.
    B. 17 Water St.
    D. 235 Spring St.

18.____

19. On the basis of the Arrest Report and paragraph above, the CORRECT entry for Box Number 14 should be
    A. 53048
    B. 31724
    C. 12/13
    D. 82460

19.____

20. On the basis of the Arrest Report and paragraph above, the CORRECT entry for Box Number 13 should be
    A. 275 Spring St.
    C. 235 Spring St.
    B. 523 River St.
    D. 17 Water St.

16.____

KEY (CORRECT ANSWERS)

1.	D	11.	D
2.	B	12.	C
3.	B	13.	C
4.	B	14.	D
5.	C	15.	B
6.	C	16.	B
7.	D	17.	A
8.	B	18.	D
9.	A	19.	D
10.	B	20.	C

MAP READING
EXAMINATION SECTION
TEST 1

DIRECTIONS: Each question or incomplete statement is followed by several suggested
answers or completions. Select the one that BEST answers the question or
completes the Statement. *PRINT THE LETTER OF THE CORRECT
ANSWER IN THE SPACE AT THE RIGHT.*

Questions 1-5.

DIRECTIONS: Questions 1 through 5 are to be answered SOLELY on the basis of the following information and map.

An employee may be required to assist civilians who seek travel directions or
referral to city agencies and facilities.

The following is a map of part of a city, where several public offices and other institutions
are located. Each of the squares represents one city block. Street names are as shown. If
there is an arrow next to the street name, it means the street is one-way only in the direction
of the arrow. If there is no arrow next to the street name, two-way traffic is allowed.

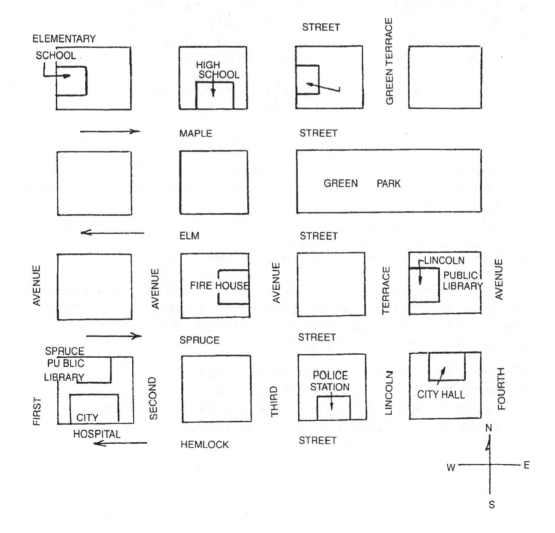

1. A woman whose handbag was stolen from her in Green Park asks a firefighter at the fire-house where to go to report the crime.
   The firefighter should tell the woman to go to the

    A. police station on Spruce Street
    B. police station on Hemlock Street
    C. city hall on Spruce Street
    D. city hall on Hemlock Street

1._____

2. A disabled senior citizen who lives on Green Terrace telephones the firehouse to ask which library is closest to her home.
   The firefighter should tell the senior citizen it is the

    A. Spruce Public Library on Lincoln Terrace
    B. Lincoln Public Library on Spruce Street
    C. Spruce Public Library on Spruce Street
    D. Lincoln Public Library on Lincoln Terrace

2._____

3. A woman calls the firehouse to ask for the exact location of City Hall.
   She should be told that it is on

    A. Hemlock Street, between Lincoln Terrace and Fourth Avenue
    B. Spruce Street, between Lincoln Terrace and Fourth Avenue
    C. Lincoln Terrace, between Spruce Street and Elm Street
    D. Green Terrace, between Maple Street and Pine Street

3._____

4. A delivery truck driver is having trouble finding the high school to make a delivery. The driver parks the truck across from the firehouse on Third Avenue facing north and goes into the firehouse to ask directions.
   In giving directions, the firefighter should tell the driver to go _____ to the school.

    A. north on Third Avenue to Pine Street and then make a right
    B. south on Third Avenue, make a left on Hemlock Street, and then make a right on Second Avenue
    C. north on Third Avenue, turn left on Elm Street, make a right on Second Avenue and go to Maple Street, then make another right
    D. north on Third Avenue to Maple Street, and then make a left

4._____

5. A man comes to the firehouse accompanied by his son and daughter. He wants to regis-ter his son in the high school and his daughter in the elementary school. He asks a fire-fighter which school is closest for him to walk to from the firehouse.
   The firefighter should tell the man that the

    A. high school is closer than the elementary school
    B. elementary school is closer than the high school
    C. elementary school and high school are the same distance away
    D. elementary school and high school are in opposite directions

5._____

Questions 6-8.

DIRECTIONS: Questions 6 through 8 are to be answered SOLELY on the basis of the following map and information. The flow of traffic is indicated by the arrows. If there
is only one arrow shown, then traffic flows in the direction indicated by the
arrow. If there are two arrows, then traffic flows in both directions. You must follow the flow of traffic

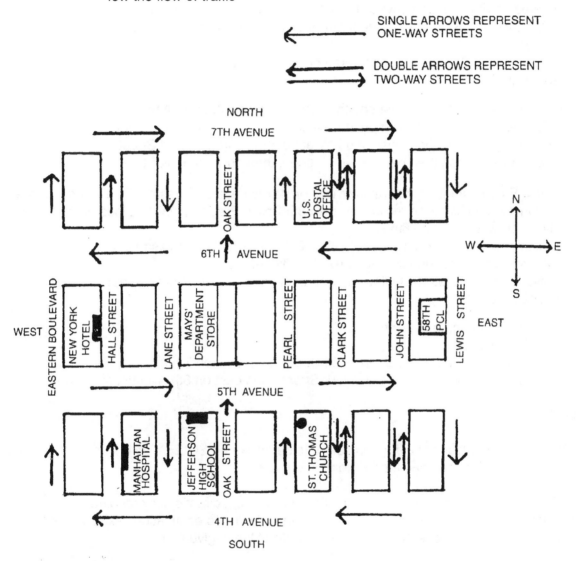

6.   Traffic Enforcement Agent Fox was on foot patrol at John Street between 6th and 7th
Avenues when a motorist driving southbound asked her for directions to the New York
Hotel, which is located on Hall Street between 5th and 6th Avenues. Which one of the fol-
lowing is the SHORTEST route for Agent Fox to direct the motorist to take, making sure
to obey all traffic regulations?
Travel _____ to the New York Hotel.

6._____

   A.   north on John Street, then east on 7th Avenue, then north on Lewis Street, then
         west on 4th Avenue, then north on Eastern Boulevard, then east on 5th Avenue,
         then north on Hall Street
   B.   south on John Street, then west on 6th Avenue, then south on Eastern Boulevard,
         then east on 5th Avenue, then north on Hall Street

    C.   south on John Street, then west on 6th Avenue, then south on Clark Street, then east on 4th Avenue, then north on Eastern Boulevard, then east on 5th Avenue, then north on Hall Street

    D.   south on John Street, then west on 4th Avenue, then north on Hall Street

7.   Traffic Enforcement Agent Murphy is on motorized patrol on 7th Avenue between Oak Street and Pearl Street when Lt. Robertson radios him to go to Jefferson High School, located on 5th Avenue between Lane Street and Oak Street. Which one of the following is the SHORTEST route for Agent Murphy to take, making sure to obey all the traffic regulations?

    Travel east on 7th Avenue, then south on _____, then east on 5th Avenue to Jefferson High School.

    7.____

    A.   Clark Street, then west on 4th Avenue, then north on Hall Street
    B.   Pearl Street, then west on 4th Avenue, then north on Lane Street
    C.   Lewis Street, then west on 6th Avenue, then south on Hall Street
    D.   Lewis Street, then west on 4th Avenue, then north on Oak Street

8.   Traffic Enforcement Agent Vasquez was on 4th Avenue and Eastern Boulevard when a motorist asked him for directions to the 58th Police Precinct, which is located on Lewis Street between 5th and 6th Avenues.

    Which one of the following is the SHORTEST route for Agent Vasquez to direct the motorist to take, making sure to obey all traffic regulations.

    Travel north on Eastern Boulevard, then east on _____ on Lewis Street to the 58th Police Precinct.

    8.____

    A.   5th Avenue, then north
    B.   7th Avenue, then south
    C.   6th Avenue, then north on Pearl Street, then east on 7th Avenue, then south
    D.   5th Avenue, then north on Clark Street, then east on 6th Avenue, then south

Questions 9-13.

DIRECTIONS: Questions 9 through 13 are to be answered SOLELY on the basis of the following map and the following information.

    Toll collectors answer motorists' questions concerning directions by reading a map of the metropolitan area. Although many alternate routes leading to destinations exist on the following map, you are to choose the MOST direct route of those given.

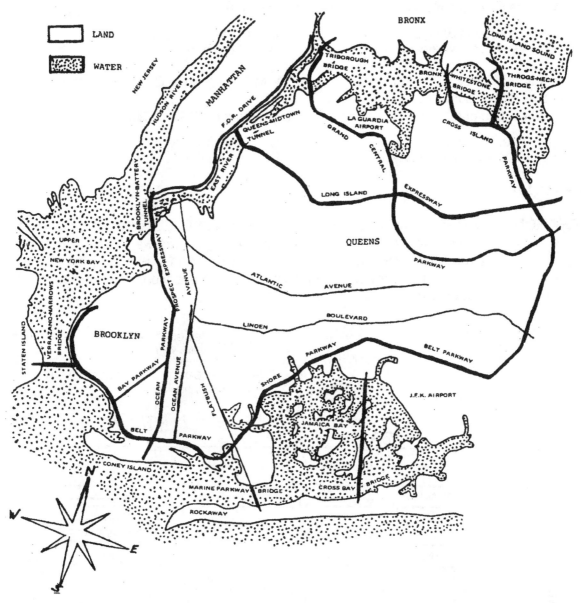

9. A motorist driving from the Bronx over the Triborough Bridge wants to go to LaGuardia Airport in Queens.
The officer should direct him to

    A. Grand Central Parkway
    C. Shore Parkway

    B. F.D.R. Drive
    D. Flatbush Avenue

9.____

10. A motorist driving from Manhattan through the Queens Midtown Tunnel would travel DIRECTLY onto

    A. Shore Parkway
    C. Long Island Expressway

    B. F.D.R. Drive
    D. Atlantic Avenue

10.____

11. A motorist traveling north over the Marine Parkway Bridge should take which route to reach Coney Island?

    A. Shore Parkway East
    C. Linden Boulevard

    B. Belt Parkway West
    D. Ocean Parkway

11.____

12. Which facility does NOT connect the Bronx and Queens?   12.____

    A. Triborough Bridge   B. Bronx-Whitestone Bridge
    C. Verrazano-Narrows Bridge   D. Throgs-Neck Bridge

13. A motorist driving from Manhattan arrives at the toll booth of the Brooklyn-Battery Tunnel   13.____
    and asks directions to Ocean Parkway.
    To which one of the following routes should the motorist FIRST be directed?

    A. Atlantic Avenue   B. Bay Parkway
    C. Prospect Expressway   D. Ocean Avenue

Questions 14-16.

DIRECTIONS: Questions 14 through 16 are to be answered SOLELY on the basis of the fol-
                    lowing map. The flow of traffic is indicated by the arrows. If there is only one
                    arrow shown, then traffic flows only in the direction indicated by the arrow. If
                    there are two arrows, then traffic flows in both directions. You must follow the
                    flow of traffic.

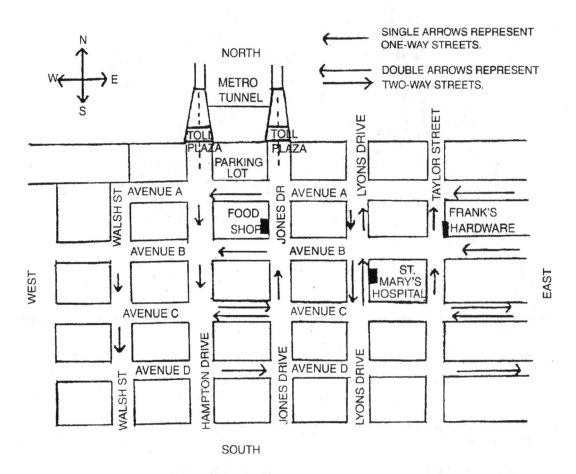

14. A motorist is exiting the Metro Tunnel and approaches the bridge and tunnel officer at the   14.____
    toll plaza. He asks the officer how to get to the food shop on Jones Drive. Which one of
    the following is the SHORTEST route for the motorist to take, making sure to obey all
    traffic regulations?
    Travel south on Hampton Drive, then left on _____ on Jones Drive to the food shop.

A.   Avenue A, then right   B.   Avenue B, then right
C.   Avenue D, then left   D.   Avenue C, then left

15.   A motorist heading south pulls up to a toll booth at the exit of the Metro Tunnel and asks   15.____
      Bridge and Tunnel Officer Evans how to get to Frank's Hardware Store on Taylor Street.
      Which one of the following is the SHORTEST route for the motorist to take, making
      sure to obey all traffic regulations?
      Travel south on Hampton Drive, then east on

      A.   Avenue B to Taylor Street
      B.   Avenue D, then north on Taylor Street to Avenue B
      C.   Avenue C, then north on Taylor Street to Avenue B
      D.   Avenue C, then north on Lyons Drive, then east on Avenue B to Taylor Street

16.   A motorist is exiting the Metro Tunnel and approaches the toll plaza. She asks Bridge   16.____
      and Tunnel Officer Owens for directions to St. Mary's Hospital.
      Which one of the following is the SHORTEST route for the motorist to take, making
      sure to obey all traffic regulations?
      Travel south on Hampton Drive, then _____ on Lyons Drive to St. Mary's Hospital.

      A.   left on Avenue D, then left
      B.   right on Avenue A, then left on Walsh Street, then left on Avenue D, then left
      C.   left on Avenue C, then left
      D.   left on Avenue B, then right

Questions 17-18.

DIRECTIONS: Questions 17 and 18 are to be answered SOLELY on the basis of the map
              which appears on the following page. The flow of traffic is indicated by the
              arrows. If there is only one arrow shown, then traffic flows only in the direction
              indicated by the arrow. If there are two arrows shown, then traffic flows in both
              directions. You must follow the flow of traffic.

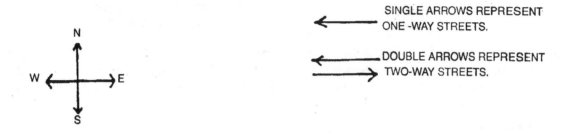

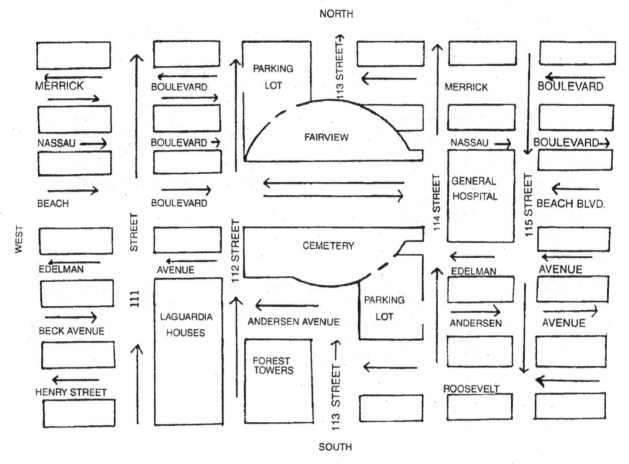

17. Police Officers Glenn and Albertson are on 111th Street at Henry Street when they are dispatched to a past robbery at Beach Boulevard and 115th Street.
Which one of the following is the SHORTEST route for the officers to follow in their patrol car, making sure to obey all traffic regulations?
Travel north on lllth Street, then east on _____ south on 115th Street.

A. Edelman Avenue, then north on 112th Street, then east on Beach Boulevard, then north on 114th Street, then east on Nassau Boulevard, then one block
B. Beach Boulevard, then north on 114th Street, then east on Nassau Boulevard, then one block
C. Merrick Boulevard, then two blocks
D. Nassau Boulevard, then south on 112th Street, then east on Beach Boulevard, then north on 114th Street, then east on Nassau Boulevard, then one block

17.____

114

18. Later in their tour, Officers Glenn and Albertson are driving on 114th Street. If they make a left turn to enter the parking lot at Andersen Avenue, and then make a u-turn, in what direction would they now be headed?

18.____

    A. North   B. South   C. East   D. West

Questions 19-20.

DIRECTIONS: Questions 19 and 20 are to be answered SOLELY on the basis of the following map. The flow of traffic is indicated by the arrows. If there is only one arrow shown, then traffic flows only in the direction indicated by the arrow. If there are two arrows shown, then traffic flows in both directions. You must follow the flow of traffic.

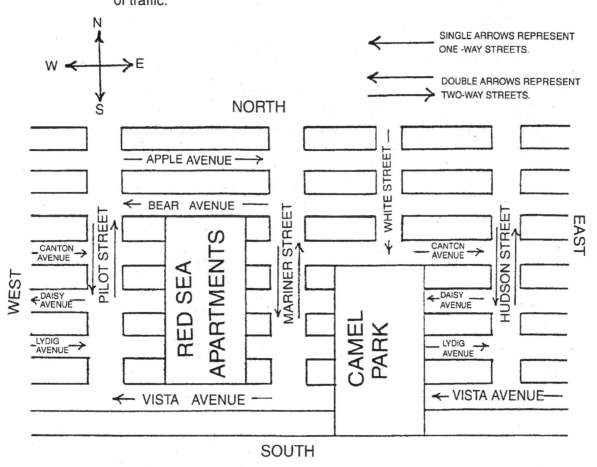

19. You are located at Apple Avenue and White Street. You receive a call to respond to the corner of Lydig Avenue and Pilot Street.
Which one of the following is the MOST direct route for you to take in your patrol car, making sure to obey all traffic regulations?
Travel _____ on Pilot Street.

19.____

    A.   two blocks south on White Street, then one block east on Canton Avenue, then one block north on Hudson Street, then three blocks west on Bear Avenue, then three blocks south

    B.   one block south on White Street, then two blocks west on Bear Avenue, then three blocks south

C. two blocks west on Apple Avenue, then four blocks south
D. two blocks south on White Street, then one block west on Canton Avenue, then three blocks south on Mariner Street, then one block west on Vista Avenue, then one block north

20. You are located at Canton Avenue and Pilot Street. You receive a call of a crime in progress at the intersection of Canton Avenue and Hudson Street.
Which one of the following is the MOST direct route for you to take in your patrol car, making sure to obey all traffic regulations?
Travel

20.____

A. two blocks north on Pilot Street, then two blocks east on Apple Avenue, then one block south on White Street, then one block east on Bear Avenue, then one block south on Hudson Street
B. three blocks south on Pilot Street, then travel one block east on Vista Avenue, then travel three blocks north on Mariner Street, then travel two blocks east on Canton Avenue
C. one block north on Pilot Street, then travel three blocks east on Bear Avenue, then travel one block south on Hudson Street
D. two blocks north on Pilot Street, then travel three blocks east on Apple Avenue, then travel two blocks south on Hudson Street

———

KEY (CORRECT ANSWERS)

1.	B		11.	B/D
2.	D		12.	C
3.	B		13.	C
4.	C		14.	D
5.	A		15.	C
6.	D		16.	C
7.	A		17.	B
8.	B		18.	C
9.	A		19.	B
10.	C		20.	D

———

EXAMINATION SECTION
TEST 1

DIRECTIONS: Each question or incomplete statement is followed by several suggested answers or completions. Select the one that BEST answers the question or completes the statement. *PRINT THE LETTER OF THE CORRECT ANSWER IN THE SPACE AT THE RIGHT.*

QUESTIONS 1-5.

The map shown on the following page represents a portion of the City of New York. Use this map to answer question 1 to 5.

1. The Verrazano Bridge is located at number   1._____

    A. 1   B. 2   C. 6   D. 17

2. Yankee Stadium is located at number   2._____

    A. 7   B. 8   C. 11   D. 15

3. The Lincoln Tunnel is located at number   3._____

    A. 2   B. 3   C. 5   D. 9

4. Kennedy Airport is located at number   4._____

    A. 4   B. 12   C. 13   D. 16

5. Coney Island is located at number   5._____

    A. 8   B. 10   C. 11   D. 14

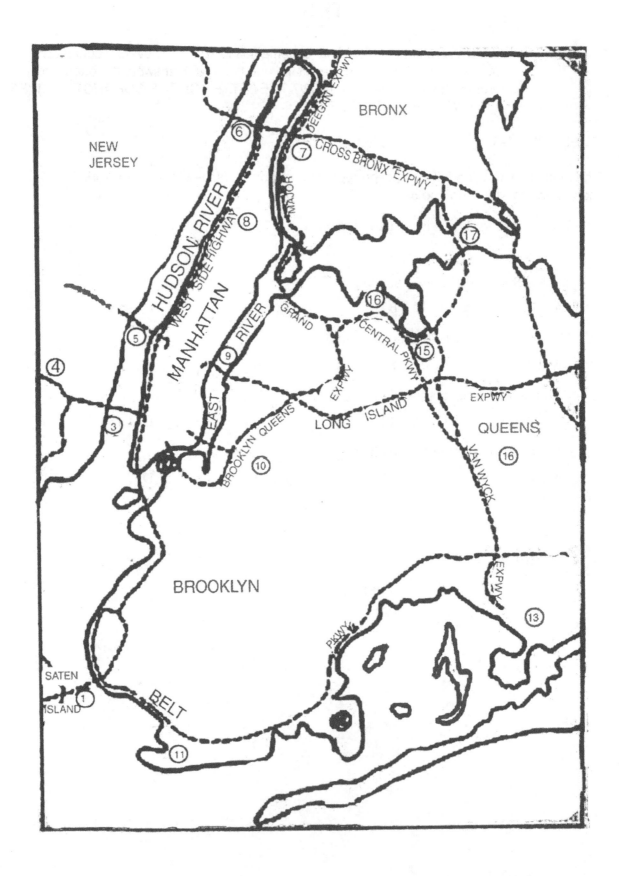

QUESTIONS 6-12.

Questions 6 to 12 deal with traffic situations which might be encountered by a Bus Operator.
In each case, select the proper action to be taken. The meaning of each symbol used in the sketches
is shown below. Note that the black dot (.) in a vehicle represents the driver of the vehicle. A vehicle not
having a black dot indicates that there is no driver in the vehicle and that the vehicle is parked at
the curb or double-parked.

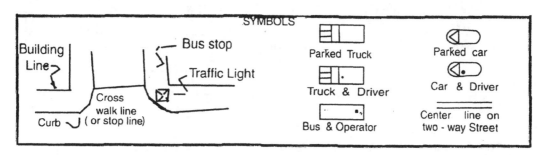

6. The vehicles on the north side of the street, including the bus, have stopped as shown because their traffic light has turned red. However, just after the Bus Operator stopped his bus, the fire alarm in the Fire House sounded, indicating that fire engines would start coming out of the Fire House. The action that the Bus Operator should IMMEDIATELY take is to

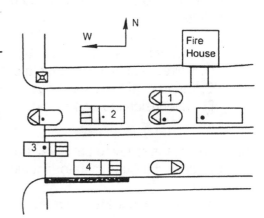

6.____

   A. pull in behind car No. 1
   B. move up alongside truck No. 2
   C. drive into the bus stop when truck No. 4 moves
   D. back up his bus under the guidance of a fireman

7. The sketch shows the condition of traffic with the buses stopped for a red light. If the indicator light on Bus No. 1 shows that it is going to make a left turn into B St., the Operator of Bus No. 2 should, when the light turns green

7.____

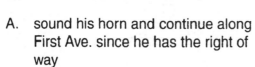

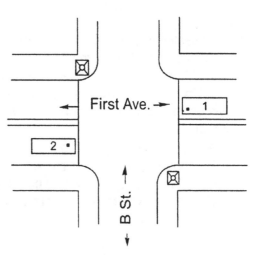

   A. sound his horn and continue along First Ave. since he has the right of way
   B. continue along his route *only* if he is behind schedule
   C. stay where he is until Bus No. 1 makes the turn since it has the right of way
   D. sound his horn and verbally warn the Operator of Bus No. 1 not to make the turn because he is in the wrong lane

8. If car No. 1 is pulling out of a parking space, the Bus Operator should

    A. sound his horn so that the car will not pull out into the traffic flow
    B. swing left over the center line to give the car ample room to pull out
    C. swing out sufficiently so as to be able to pass car No. 1
    D. slow up and let car No. 1 pull out

8.____

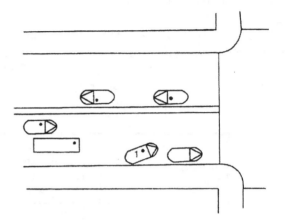

9. If the Bus Operator sees that there is a parked car in the bus stop, he should open his doors for the discharge of passengers

    A. where he is
    B. directly behind the parked car
    C. in front of the parked car
    D. alongside the parked car

9.____

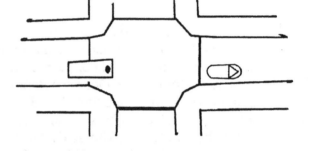

10. If the bus is ready to pull away from the bus stop, the Bus Operator should

    A. pull out quickly before car No. 4 blocks the way
    B. pull up behind car No. 2
    C. wait until car No. 4 passes before pulling out
    D. wait until car No. 2 moves on

10.____

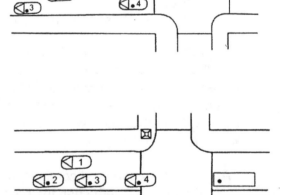

11. The sketch shows the condition of traffic just before the light turns green for the bus. There is traffic congestion ahead of car No. 2 which prevents it from moving. When the light turns green the Bus Operator should

    A. pull in behind car No. 1
    B. drive up beside car No. 4
    C. slowly creep up behind car No. 4
    D. remain where he is until car No. 4 moves up

11.____

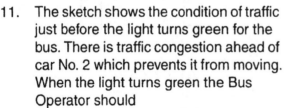

12. The bus shown in the sketch is traveling at twenty miles per hour along Main Street. If the traffic light for the bus turned from green to yellow when the bus reached the location shown, it would be BEST for the Bus Operator to

12.____

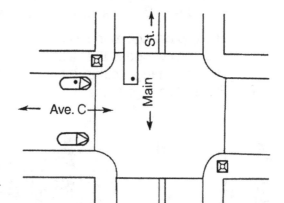

    A. stop where he is
    B. turn right into Ave. C
    C. wait until the cars on Ave. C pass, then proceed
    D. continue past the light, without stopping

QUESTIONS 13-21.

Questions 13-21 refer to the Bus Map on the following page which shows the routes of various buses. The Bus Route Number is shown by a number within a box (R-2)and the route followed by the bus is shown as a box a broken line(■ ■ ■ ■) Use this map to answer questions 13 to 21.

13. If you are at the Tunnel located in the lower right part of the map and want to go MOST directly to the Skating Rink located in the upper left part of the map, you should take bus number

13.____

    A. R-12   B. R-14   C. R-16   D. R-18

14. If you are at Main St. and 29th St. and want to go MOST directly to the World Court at 18th St. and Ave. B you should take bus number

14.____

    A. R-5   B. R-7   C. R-9   D. R-11

15. If you are at the Bridge located on the upper right side of the map and want to go MOST directly to the Medical Center at 9th St. and Ave. B, you should take bus number

15.____

    A. R-2   B. R-4   C. R-6   D. R-8

16. If you are at the Tunnel located in the lower right part of the map and want to go MOST directly to the Museum at 44th St. and Ave. H, you should take bus number

16.____

    A. R-12   B. R-14   C. R-16   D. R-18

17. If you are at Main St. and 28th St. and want to go MOST directly to Union Station at 22nd St. and Ave. F, you should take bus number

17.____

    A. R-5   B. R-7   C. R-9   D. R-ll

18. If you are at the Bridge located in the upper right side of the map and want to go MOST directly to the Sports garden at 10th St. and Ave. J, you should take bus number

18.____

    A. R-6   B. R-7   C. R-9   D. R-18

19. If you leave the Sports Garden at 10th St. and Ave. J and want to go MOST directly to 44th St. and Ave. B, you should take bus number

19.____

    A.   R-7 and change to the R-10
    B.   R-8 and change to the R-12
    C.   R-9 and change to the R-14
    D.   R-6 and change to the R-12

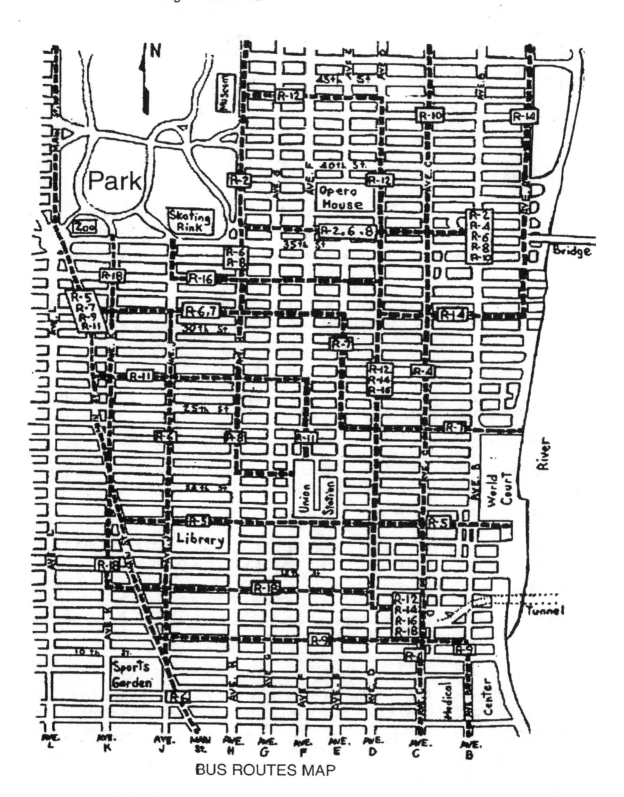

BUS ROUTES MAP

20. If you leave Union Station at Ave. F and 18th St. and want to go MOST directly to the   20.____
Museum at 44th St. and Ave. H, you should take bus number

    A. R-11 and change to the R-8
    B. R-11 and change to the R-6
    C. R-5 and change to the R-2
    D. R-5 and change to the R-12

21. If you leave the Opera House at Ave. D and 37th St. and want to go MOST directly to the   21.____
Zoo in the Park located in the upper left side of the map, you should take bus number

    A. R-12 and change to the R-16
    B. R-12 and change to the R-11
    C. R-6 and change to the R-16
    D. R-8 and change to the R-7

22. At the scene of a bus accident, a Bus Operator is questioned by a man claiming to be a   22.____
newspaper reporter. The Bus Operator would be using good judgment if he

    A. cooperates fully with the reporter since this would show good will on the part of the
transit authority
    B. first checks the reporter's credentials and then gives him any information which will
eventually be included in a transit authority accident report
    C. gives the desired information *only* on the understanding that he will NOT be quoted
    D. refers the reporter to the proper officials of the transit authority

QUESTIONS 23-25.

Questions 23-25 deal with descriptions of various types of motor vehicle accidents. In each of
these questions, select the sketch which most accurately represents the word description of the
accident given in the question. The meaning of each symbol given in the sketches is shown
below.

23. Car #2 and the bus were proceeding **north** on Ave. M, with Car #2 tailgating the bus. Car   23.__
#1 was **proceeding east** on Peck St. When the bus stopped suddenly to **avoid hitting** Car
#1, it was immediately struck from behind by Car #2. Car #1 continued **east** on Peck St.
while both Car #2 and the bus stopped after the collision.

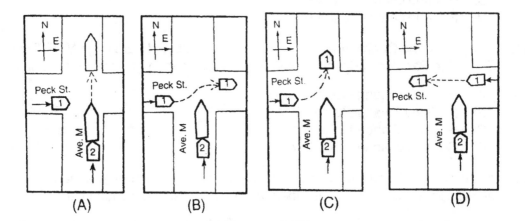

(A)   (B)   (C)   (D)

24. Mr. Jones was crossing Baker Street when he was struck by a bus approaching from his   24.__
right. After hitting Mr. Jones, the bus swerved left and ran into a tree.

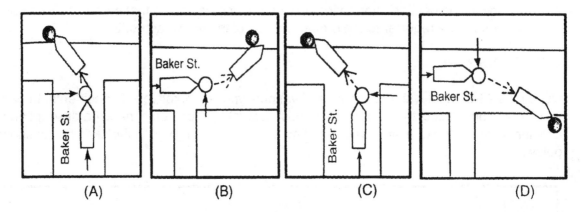

(A)   (B)   (C)   (D)

25. While a Bus Operator was driving his bus on a two-way street, a child suddenly ran out in   25.__
front of the bus from between two parked cars. To avoid hitting the child, the Bus Operator swung his bus sharply to the left. By so doing, the bus crossed the center line and
crashed head-on into an oncoming car. The collision caused the car to swing to the right
and into the curb.

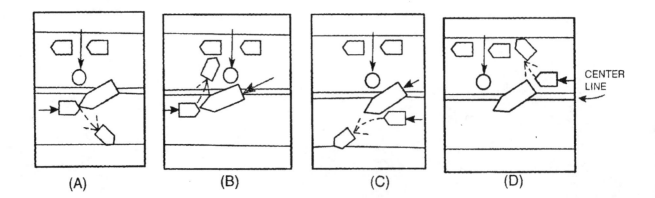

(A)   (B)   (C)   (D)

KEY (CORRECT ANSWERS)

1.	A		11.	D
2.	A		12.	D
3.	C		13.	C
4.	C		14.	A
5.	C		15.	B
6.	D		16.	A
7.	A		17.	D
8.	D		18.	A
9.	C		19.	D
10.	C		20.	D

21.	D
22.	D
23.	B
24.	A
25.	A

CPSIA information can be obtained
at www.ICGtesting.com
Printed in the USA
BVHW021254070123
655806BV00011B/202